UPDATED EDITION

Guess What!

Activity Book 4
with Digital Pack

British English

Lynne Marie Robertson
Series Editor: Lesley Koustaff

CAMBRIDGE

CAMBRIDGE
UNIVERSITY PRESS & ASSESSMENT

Shaftesbury Road, Cambridge CB2 8EA, United Kingdom

One Liberty Plaza, 20th Floor, New York, NY 10006, USA

477 Williamstown Road, Port Melbourne, VIC 3207, Australia

314–321, 3rd Floor, Plot 3, Splendor Forum, Jasola District Centre, New Delhi – 110025, India

103 Penang Road, #05–06/07, Visioncrest Commercial, Singapore 238467

Cambridge University Press & Assessment is a department of the University of Cambridge.

It furthers the University's mission by disseminating knowledge in the pursuit of education, learning and research at the highest international levels of excellence.

www.cambridge.org
Information on this title: www.cambridge.org/9781009798341

First published 2014
Updated edition 2024

20 19 18 17 16 15 14 13 12 11 10 9 8 7 6

Printed in Poland by Opolgraf

A catalogue record for this publication is available from the British Library

ISBN 978-1-009-79834-1 Activity Book with Digital Pack Level 4
ISBN 978-1-009-79830-3 Pupil's Book with eBook Level 4
ISBN 978-1-009-79841-9 Teacher's Book with Digital Pack Level 4
ISBN 978-1-107-54546-5 Flashcards Level 4

Additional resources for this publication at www.cambridge.org/guesswhatue

Contents

Welcome back!

1 Look and write the number.

1
2
3
4
5
6

curly hair	straight hair	fair hair	red hair	dark hair	glasses
					1

2 Look and write the words.

1 He's got ___short___ hair.
2 He's got ______ hair.
3 He's got ______ hair.
4 He's got ______ .
5 She's got ___long___ hair.
6 She's got ______ .
7 She's got ______ hair.
8 She's got ______ hair.

3 Think Look at activity 2. Write the words.

How are they the same?	How are they different?
1 He's got ___curly___ hair. She's got ___curly___ hair. 2 He's got ______ . She's got ______ .	3 He's got ______ hair. She's got ______ hair. 4 He's got ______ hair. She's got ______ hair.

My picture dictionary → Go to page 84: Find and write the new words.

4 Read and match.

a

b

c

d

e

1 She's tall. She's got short straight hair. ___b___
2 He's short. He's got big glasses. ______
3 She's tall. She's got long straight hair. ______
4 He's short. He's got small glasses. ______
5 She's short. She's got curly red hair. ______

5 Look and complete the questions and answers.

Tim
Helen
Simon
Laura

1 (Tim) What does ___he look like?___
______ tall. ______ short fair hair and big glasses.
2 (Helen) What does ______ ?
______ short. ______ short curly hair and small glasses.
3 (Simon) What does ______ ?
______ short. ______ curly dark hair and small sunglasses.
4 (Laura) What does ______ ?
______ tall. ______ straight red hair and big sunglasses.

6 About Me Write about a person in your family.

My ... has got ... hair ______

______

______

7 Think Look and match. Then write the answers.

86 cm ~~1 m 23 cm~~ 28 cm 1 m 55 cm 64 cm

1 How tall is the boy? *He's 1 metre 23 centimetres.*

2 How high is the chair? *It's* ____________________

3 How tall is the girl? ____________________

4 How tall is the rabbit? ____________________

5 How high is the guitar? ____________________

8 About Me Answer the questions.

1 How tall is your friend? ____________________

2 How tall is your mum/dad? ____________________

3 How tall are you? ____________________

4 How high is your chair? ____________________

Skills: *Writing*

9 Read the paragraph and write the words.

dark short ~~1 m 22 cm~~ cinema blue playing 71 cm bike

My friend's name is Paul. He's [1] *1 m 22 cm* tall.
He's got [2] ______ [3] ______ hair.
He likes [4] ______ football. He's got a
[5] ______ [6] ______. It's [7] ______ high.
He likes going to the [8] ______ on Saturdays.

1m 22cm
71cm

10 About Me Answer the questions.

1 What's your friend's name?
My friend's name is ______
2 How tall is your friend?
______
3 What does your friend look like?
______
4 What sports does your friend like?
______
5 What activities does your friend like doing?
______

11 About Me Write about your friend.

My friend's ______
______
______

12 About Me Think of a friend. Ask and answer with another friend.

What does your friend look like? She's got fair hair and glasses.

Is it Mary? Yes, it is!

13 Read and match.

1 Let's register now!
2 ~~No, let's watch TV.~~
3 We all like adventures.
4 Do you want to help your local community?

a

What shall we do this afternoon?
How about swimming?
2

b

____
34
I do! I do!
Anna! Sit down.

c

We're making a new adventure playground. Register online for the free app.
How exciting! ____

d

What shall we call our team?
How about the Adventurers? ____ .
Good idea.

14 Look at activity 13. Circle the answers.

1 They want to ______________ .
a play in the rain   b go swimming   c (watch TV)

2 *Daisy does it!* is the name of ______________ .
a their friend   b their community   c a TV programme

3 The TV programme asks them to ______________ .
a make a new supermarket   b help their community
c make a new school

4 They register to ______________ .
a get a free app   b watch TV   c sit down

5 The Adventurers is the name of ______________ .
a their team   b the local community   c the new playground

15 Read and tick the activities that show the value: get involved with your local community.

1 help make a playground ✓

2 ride your bike ☐

3 pick up litter ☐

4 go to school ☐

5 read a book ☐

6 clean the beach ☐

16 Find and tick the words that sound like *owl*.

1

a

✓

b

✓

c

2

a

b

c

3

a

b

c

4

a

b

c

What patterns can you see?

1 Look and read. Circle the patterns you can see.

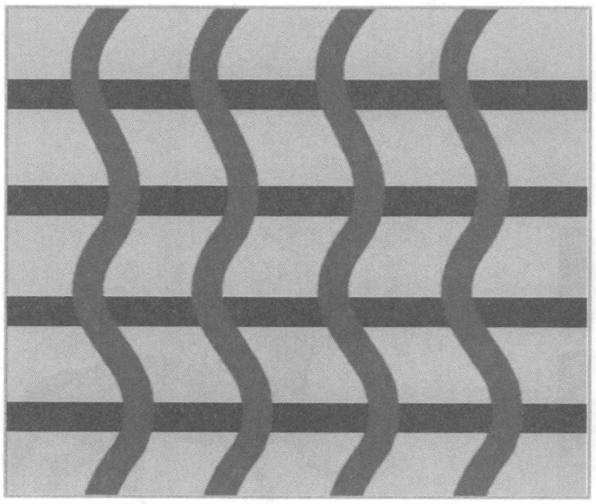

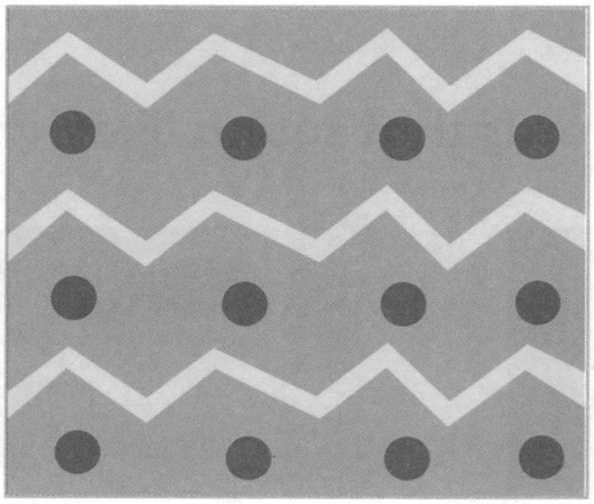

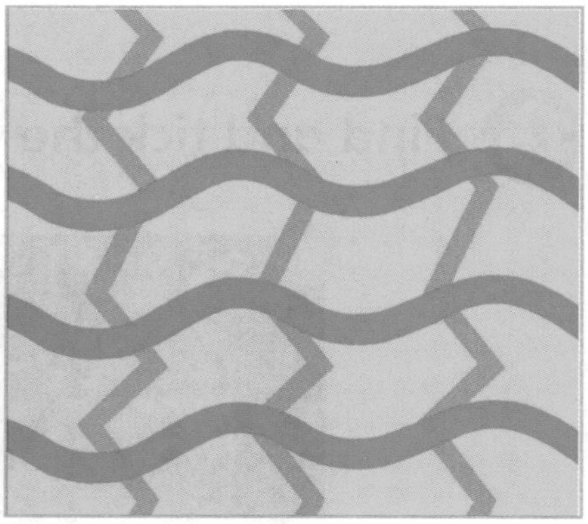

1 zigzags and wavy lines
wavy lines and stripes
stripes and zigzags

2 spots and stripes
wavy lines and spots
zigzags and spots

3 wavy lines and stripes
stripes and zigzags
zigzags and wavy lines

2 Read and draw.

1
Draw four green zigzags at the top.
Draw six red stripes under the zigzags.
Draw two purple spots under the stripes.

2
Draw a circle.
Draw nine blue spots in the circle.
Draw three orange stripes next to the circle.

3
Draw a big square.
Draw seven yellow stripes in the square.
Draw six black wavy lines between the stripes.

Evaluation

1 Look and write the questions and answers. Then match.

1 What does Sally *look* *like* ?

2 What does Herman ______ ______ ?

3 What does Macy ______ ______ ?

4 What does Raul ______ ______ ?

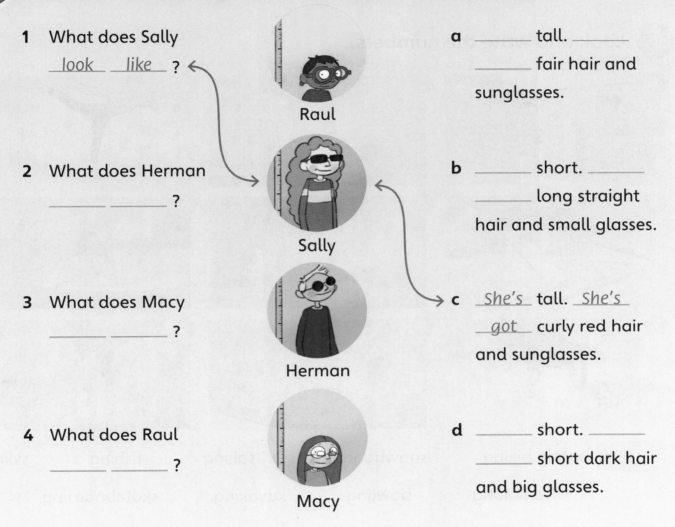

Raul

Sally

Herman

Macy

a ______ tall. ______ ______ fair hair and sunglasses.

b ______ short. ______ ______ long straight hair and small glasses.

c *She's* tall. *She's* *got* curly red hair and sunglasses.

d ______ short. ______ ______ short dark hair and big glasses.

2 About Me Complete the sentences about this unit.

1 I can talk about ______________ .

2 I can write about ______________ .

3 My favourite part is ______________ .

3 Puzzle Guess what it is.

Hair that's not straight.

What is it? ______________

Go to page 93 and write the answer.

1 Fun sports

1 Look and write the numbers.

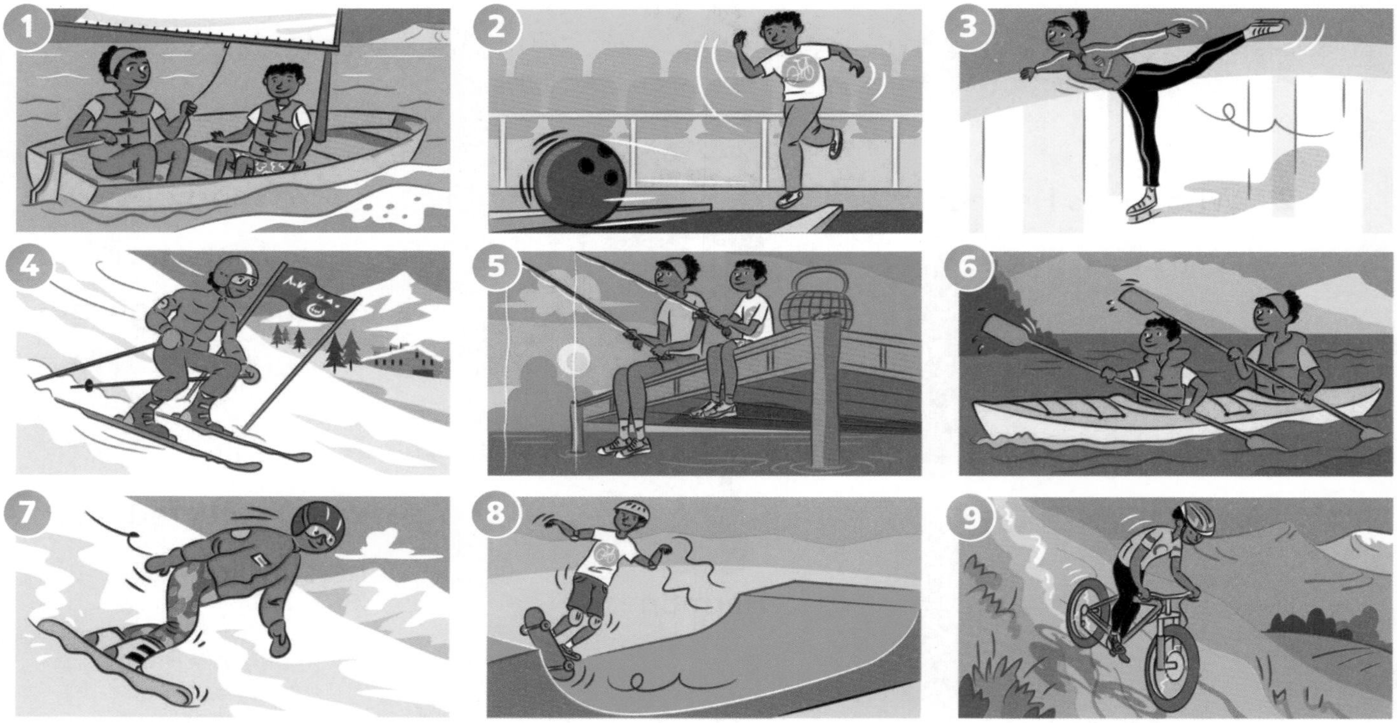

[ ] mountain biking [ ] snowboarding [1] sailing [ ] fishing [ ] skiing

[ ] ice skating [ ] bowling [ ] kayaking [ ] skateboarding

2 Think Where do you do the sports? Look at activity 1 and write.

river/sea 	mountain 	city/town 
1 sailing	4 ______	7 ______
2 ______	5 ______	8 ______
3 ______	6 ______	9 ______

My picture dictionary → Go to page 85: Find and write the new words.

3 Look and read. Then circle.

1 He's / He isn't very good at kayaking.
2 She's / She isn't good at mountain biking.
3 He's / He isn't good at skateboarding.
4 He's / He isn't very good at ice skating.
5 She's / She isn't good at skiing.

4 Look and write the words.

1

I'm not very good at skateboarding .

2

________ good at ice skating.

3

________ very good at ________ .

4

____

5 Complete the conversations.

1

Are you good at bowling?
Yes, I am .

2

________ good at ice skating?
No, ________ .

3

________ good at?
________ good at playing the piano.

6 Think Look and write.

Ben 	mountain biking ✗	guitar ✓	**Liz** 	kayaking ✓	violin ✗

1 **Ben:** Are you good at playing the violin? **Liz:** No, I'm not.

2 **Liz:** ________ good at mountain biking?

Ben: ________

3 **Ben:** ________ good at?

Liz: ________ good at ________ .

4 **Liz:** ________ good at?

Ben: ________ good at ________ .

7 About Me Answer the questions.

1 Are you good at music? ________

2 Are you good at skiing? ________

3 What are you good at? ________

4 What are you not very good at? ________

5 What do you want to be good at? ________

Skills: *Writing*

8 About Me Read and answer. Circle *yes* or *no*.

Are you good at … ?

Music	yes	no	making films	yes	no
Art	yes	no	playing table tennis	yes	no
dancing	yes	no	gymnastics	yes	no
singing	yes	no	karate	yes	no
playing the piano	yes	no	playing the guitar	yes	no

9 Ask three friends. Write their name and answers.

What are you good at?

I'm good at singing.

Name:	Good at:
______________	______________
______________	______________
______________	______________

10 Look at activities 8 and 9. Plan a talent show.

Talent show!

Time: 6 o'clock
Place: gym

1. Heidi's good at singing. And she can dance.
2. Jim's good at playing the guitar.
3. Me – I'm good at making films about karate.

Talent show!

Time: ______________

Place: ______________

1 ______________

2 ______________

3 ______________

11 Read and number in order.

a

Who wants to help paint the wall?
I do! I'm good at painting.
So are we, Anna! Let's all help.

b

It looks great. Well done!
It's me!

c

Wait and see, Anna.
Who are you painting, Lily?

d

Red hair and green eyes. Good!
Can I see?
Shh, Anna!

e

Welcome to Pinton Woods! I'm Daisy.
Hello. We're the Adventurers.

f

Thanks, Grandma!
We don't need this paint. Here you are.
1

12 Look at activity 11. Answer the questions.

1 Who gives paint to the children? Grandma.

2 What do the children help to paint? ____________

3 Are the children good at painting? ____________

4 Who does Lily paint? ____________

5 Does Daisy like the wall painting? ____________

13 Look and tick the picture that shows the value: allow others to work.

1

2

159
× 3

3

14 Find and tick the words that sound like *coil*.

1

a

b

c

2

a

b

c

3

a

b
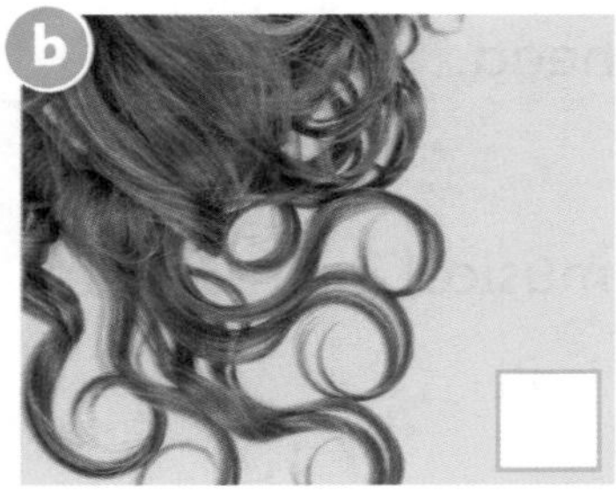

c

What type of body movements can we make?

1 What body movements can you see? Circle the correct words.

1 stretch, bend, kick
kick, bend, stretch
bend, stretch, kick

2 turn, stretch, shake
shake, stretch, turn
bend, stretch, turn

3 shake, bend, kick
kick, shake, turn
shake, turn, bend

2 Complete the sentences with body movements.

1 She can b e n d her body.
2 He can _ _ _ _ his head.
3 She wants to _ _ _ _ _ _ _ his legs.
4 Let's _ _ _ _ _ the musical instruments.
5 He can _ _ _ _ the ball.

Evaluation

1 Look and write.

1

What are you good at?
I'm good at making models.

2

What are you good at?
_______________ good at skiing.

3

____
____

4

____
____

5

____
____

2 About Me Complete the sentences about this unit.

1 I can talk about _______________ .

2 I can write about _______________ .

3 My favourite part is _______________ .

3 Puzzle Guess what it is.

You need water and wind to do this sport. What is it? _______________

Go to page 93 and write the answer.

2 Around town

1 Look and number the picture.

1

1 ~~shopping centre~~
2 underground station
3 bus station
4 restaurant
5 square
6 bank

2 Think Read and match. Then write the words.

1 It means *stop* and *go*. It's red, yellow and green.
2 It's black and white. It's not an animal.
3 I can eat here.
4 I can sleep here.
5 I can see art here.

museum
restaurant
~~traffic light~~
hotel
zebra crossing

a 
b 
c 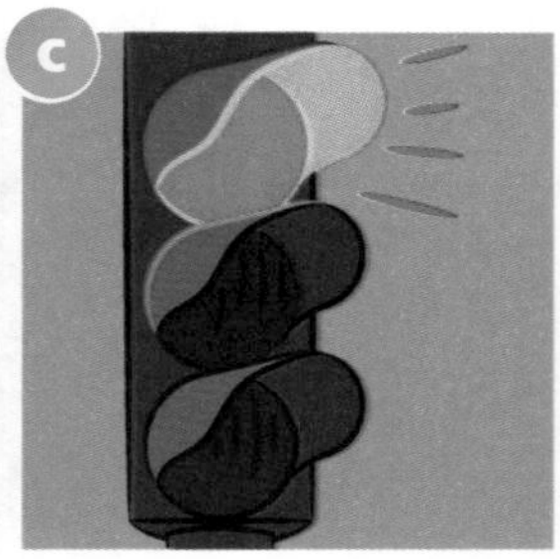
d 
e 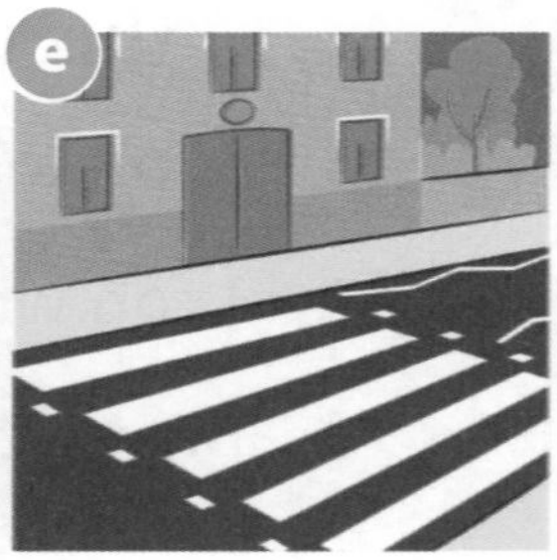

a ______ b ______ c *traffic light* d ______ e ______

My picture dictionary → Go to page 86: Find and write the new words.

3 Look and circle the correct answers.

HOTEL
HOTEL
MUSEUM

1 Where's the restaurant?
It's .... the hotel.
a (above) b opposite c below

2 Where's the museum?
It's .... the traffic light.
a below b opposite c far from

3 Where's the underground station?
It's .... the hotel.
a below b next to c above

4 Where's the shopping centre?
It's .... the museum.
a opposite b next to c far from

5 Where's the bank?
It's .... the zebra crossing.
a near b below c far from

4 Look at activity 3. Complete the questions and answers.

1 *Where's* the train?
It's *next to* the hotel.

2 ____________ the helicopter?
It's ____________ the bank.

3 ____________ the car?
It's ____________ the shopping centre.

4 ____________ the train?
It's ____________ the plane.

5 ____________ the traffic light?
It's ____________ the zebra crossing.

5 Think Read and draw lines. Then answer the questions.

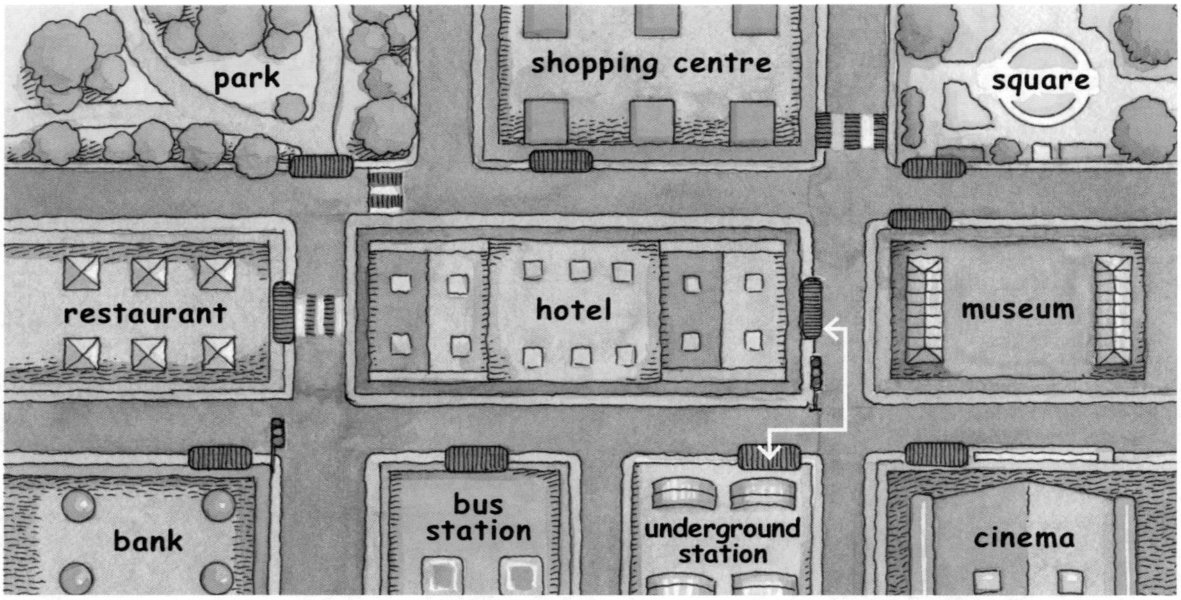
park
shopping centre
square
restaurant
hotel
museum
bank
bus station
underground station
cinema

1 Start at the underground station. Turn right. Turn left at the traffic light. It's on the left. Where are you?

hotel

2 Start at the restaurant. Turn right. Turn left. It's on the right, opposite the hotel. Where are you?

____

3 Start at the park. Cross the first zebra crossing. Turn left. Go straight ahead. It's on the right, opposite the square. Where are you?

____

4 Start at the shopping centre. Turn right and go straight ahead. Turn left at the zebra crossing. Go straight ahead. Turn right at the zebra crossing. Stop. Where are you?

____

5 Start at the square. Turn right. Turn left. Go straight ahead. Turn left after the museum. Stop. Where are you?

____

6 Look at activity 5. Write the directions.

1 Where's the museum? Start at the bank. Turn ________________

2 Where's the bus station? Start at the square. ________________

3 Where's the park? Start at the cinema. ________________

Skills: *Writing*

7 Read the paragraph and write the words.

museum   restaurants   ~~square~~   shopping centre   station

My favourite city

My favourite city is Tokyo in Japan. You can see a statue of a famous dog, Hachiko, in a [1] *square* . I like eating at cafés and [2] ________________ there too. I also like going shopping in Harajuku. You can see lots of beautiful clothes at the [3] ________________ .

Yoyogi Park is next to the underground [4] ________________ . You can see bands playing music. It's very exciting!

The art [5] ________________ is opposite the park on the left. You can see old Japanese art there.

8 About Me Answer the questions.

1 What's your favourite city?

____

2 What do you like doing there?

____

3 Where do you like going?

____

4 What can you see there?

____

9 About Me Write about your favourite city or town.

My favourite city is ____

____

____

____

10 About Me Ask and answer with a friend.

What's your favourite city?

My favourite city is Madrid.

11 Read and match.

1 Stop at the traffic lights.
2 Turn left at the museum and go straight ahead.
3 Can we have the net, please?
4 ~~I know. Follow me.~~

a

Look at this! A net!
Football competition Harton Park
How many goals can you score?
Where's Harton?
4

b

Be careful everyone.
Yes, OK.

c

Excuse me. How do you get to the park?
Thanks.
MUSEUM

d

It's for the adventure playground.
OK!

12 Look at activity 11. Write *yes* or *no*.

1 The museum is near the park. *yes*
2 Tom knows where Harton is. ______
3 It is safe to stop at the traffic lights. ______
4 They turn right at the museum. ______
5 They get a net at the park. ______

13 **Look and tick the pictures that show the value: cycle safely.**

1
a
b
✓
2
a
b
3
a
b

14 **Colour the words that sound like *surf*. Then answer the question.**

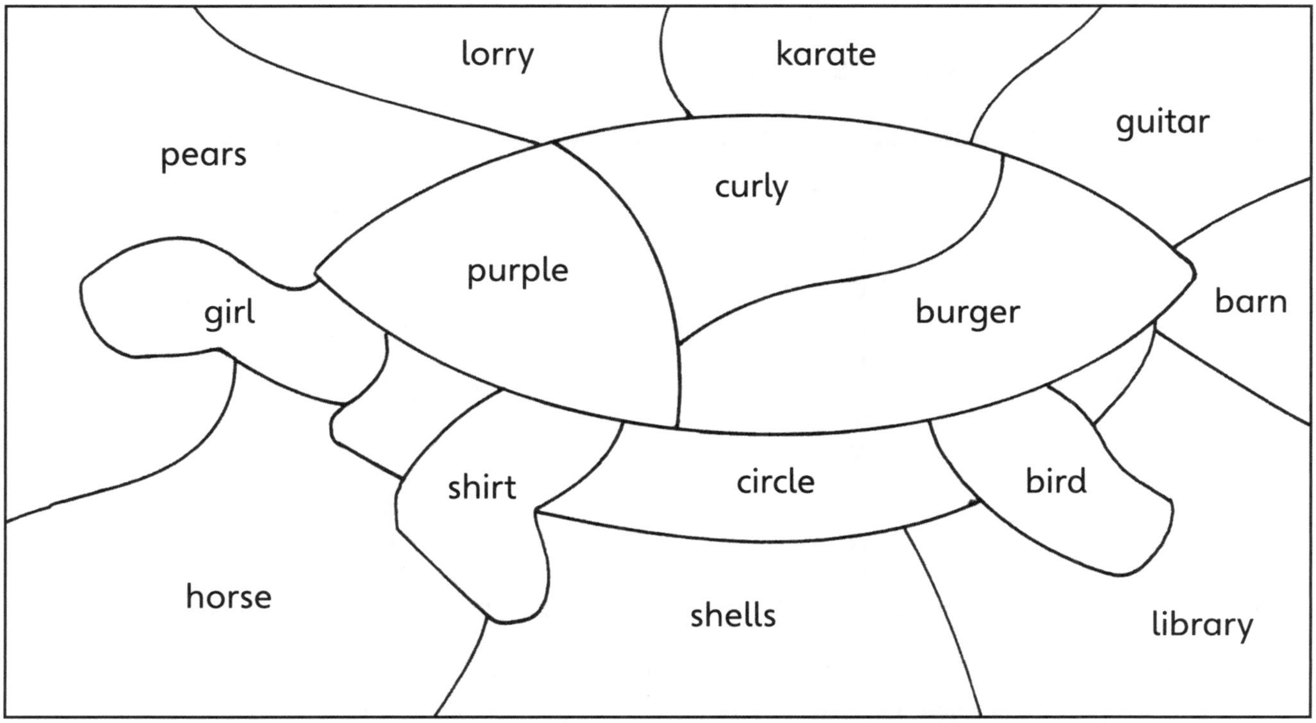
lorry
karate
guitar
pears
curly
purple
barn
girl
burger
shirt
circle
bird
horse
shells
library

What is it? ______________________________

What 3D shapes can you see?

1 Read and match.

1 There are four cylinders. b
2 There's a big cube and a small pyramid.
3 There's a big sphere and four small spheres.
4 There are four small cones and a pyramid.
5 There are four small cones and a cube.

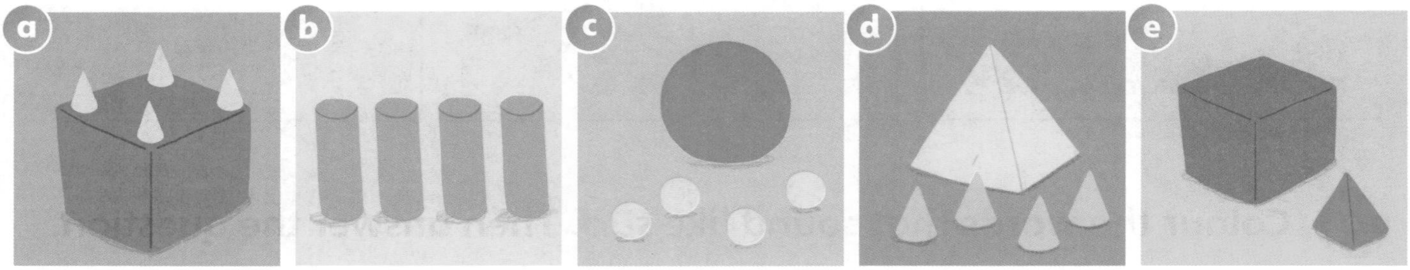
a
b
c
d
e

2 Draw the 3D shapes.

1

2

3

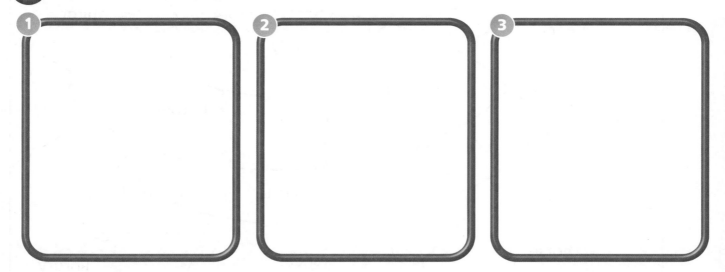

1 Draw a museum. It's a cube. It's got two cone shapes and five cylinders.
2 Draw an underground station. It's a cylinder. It's got eight spheres and three pyramids.
3 Draw a hotel. It's a pyramid. It's got a cube at the front and a sphere on top.

Evaluation

1 Look and complete the questions and answers.

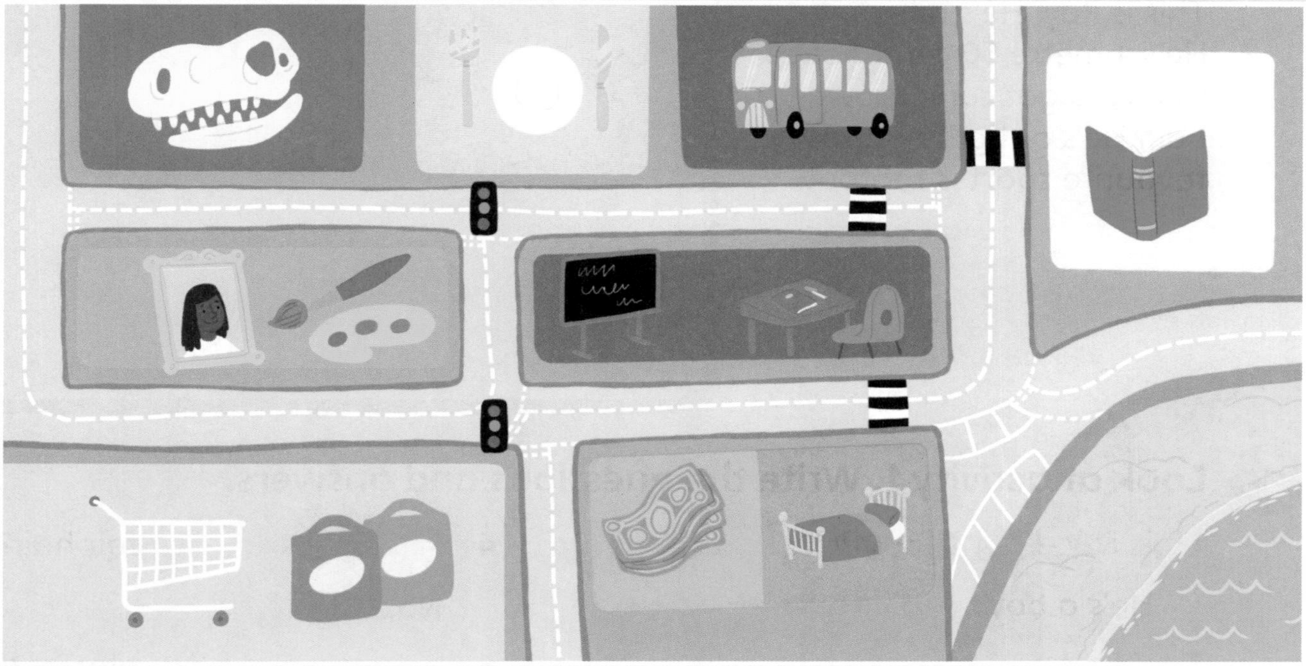

1 Where's the bank?

It's next to the hotel.

2 Where's the art gallery?

It's __________ the museum.

3 Where's the shopping centre?

It's __________ the book shop.

4 Where's the restaurant?

It's __________ the bus station.

2 About Me Complete the sentences about this unit.

1 I can talk about __________ .

2 I can write about __________ .

3 My favourite part is __________ .

3 Puzzle Guess what it is.

You stop when it's red. You go when it's green. What is it?

____

Go to page 93 and write the answer.

Review Units 1 and 2

1 Read and draw.

This is Ray. He's a boy.
He's **1** metre 50 centimetres tall. He's got curly brown hair. He's got glasses. His favourite sport is football.

2 Look at activity 1. Write the questions and answers.

1 *Is Ray a boy or a girl?*

He's a boy.

2 ______________________

He's **1** metre 50 centimetres.

3 ______________________ ?

He's tall. He's got curly hair.

4 ______________ fair hair?

No, ______________ .

5 ______________ glasses?

Yes, ______________ .

6 ______________ football?

Yes, ______________ .

3 Look and write.

1 Me

I'm *not very good at ice skating* .

2 Me

STRIKE!

______________ good at ______________ .

3 Henri

He's ______________________ .

4 Lori

She's ______________________ .

4 About Me Look at activity 3 and write about you.

1 I'm __________ at ice skating.

2 I'm __________ at bowling.

3 ______________________

4 ______________________

5 Look and complete the questions and answers. Then match.

[3] *Are you good at singing?*

No, __________ .

[ ] __________ good at playing the piano?

Yes, __________ .

[ ] __________ good at playing the recorder?

Yes, __________ .

[ ] __________ good at playing the guitar?

No, __________ .

1
2
3
4
H

6 Think Do the word puzzle. Then use the letters in the circles to answer the question.

Across →

1
2
3
4
5
6

Down ↓

7
8
9
10

1 bus station
2
3
4
5
6
7
8
9
10

Which letter of the alphabet has got lots of w _ _ _ _ ? The ' ______ ' (sea).

3 At work

1 Think Write the words. Then tick the odd one out.

~~actor~~
actor
artist
bus driver
businessman
businesswoman
~~doctor~~
~~nurse~~
pilot
singer
singer
vet

1

 ✓

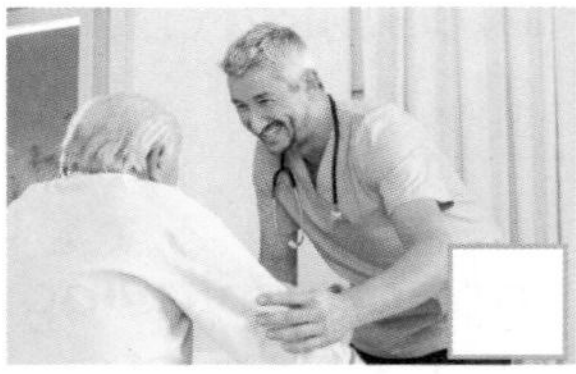

actor | *doctor* | *nurse*

2

______ | ______ | ______

3

______ | ______ | ______

4

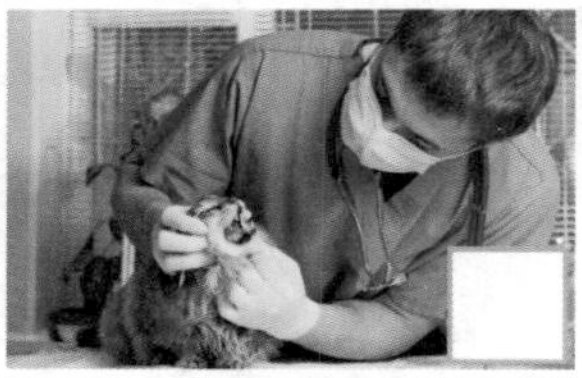

______ | ______ | ______

2 Look at activity 1. Write the words.

Where do they work?		
in a hospital	in an office	in a theatre
doctor		

My picture dictionary → Go to page 87: Find and write the new words.

3 Put the words in order. Then match.

1 do / your / What / does / dad / ?

What does your dad do?

2 aunt / does / do / your / What / ?

____

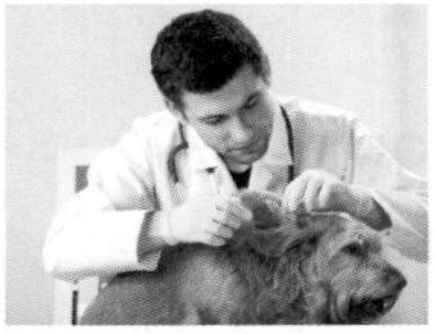

3 do / your / does / uncle / What / ?

____

4 does / mum / What / do / your / ?

____

She's / businesswoman / a / .

____

vet / a / He's / .

____

a / She's / pilot / .

____

actor / He's / an / .

He's an actor.

4 Look at activity 3. Complete the questions and answers.

1 (your uncle) *Where does* he *work?*

He works in an animal hospital.

2 (your aunt) ______________ she ______________ ?

______________ in a plane.

3 (your dad) ______________ he ______________ ?

____

4 (your mum) ______________ she ______________ ?

____

5 Write the name of a famous person. Then ask and answer with a friend.

What does she do? She's a singer.

Where does she work? She works in theatres and studios.

6 Read and number.

1

1 I want to be a pilot.
2 I want to be a bus driver.
3 I want to be a businesswoman.
4 I want to be an actor.
5 I want to be a farmer.

7 Look and write the questions and answers.

1 What do you *want to be?*

I *want to be* a doctor.

2 ______________________

____

3 What do you ______________ ?

I ______________ a singer.

2+2=

4 ______________________

____

8 About Me Answer the questions.

1 Do you want to be a vet?

____

2 Do you want to be a footballer?

____

3 Do you want to be a pilot?

____

4 What do you want to be?

____

Skills: *Writing*

9 Read the paragraph and write the words.

~~want to~~ Maths like office don't planes want to

I [1] *want to* be a pilot. I [2] ______ seeing new things and I like learning about new places. I'm good at [3] ______ . I [4] ______ want to work in an [5] ______ . I [6] ______ work on a plane and fly in the sky. I want to work with [7] ______ !

10 About Me Answer the questions.

1 What do you want to be?

______

2 What do you like doing?

______

3 What are you good at?

______

4 Where do you want to work?

______

5 Who/What do you want to work with?

______

11 About Me Write about what you want to be.

I want to be ______

______

______

______

______

12 About Me Ask and answer with a friend.

What do you want to be?

I want to be a farmer.

13 Read and write the words.

Yes, please. ~~farmer~~ don't need to animals Shall I farm help me

a
Let's ask my uncle. He's a farmer. He's got some on his farm.
b
Hi, Uncle Jim. Can we have some rope and tyres, please?
What for?
For the adventure playground.
OK, but can you ________ with the ________ first?
c
________ feed the hens?
OK!
________ . Lucas, can you give some water to the horse?
d
Shall I take the dog for a walk?
We ________ , Anna. Let's look at the goats.

14 Look at activity 13. Circle the answers.

1 Lily's uncle is a ________ .
 a (farmer) b rope c tyre

2 The ropes and tyres are for ________ .
 a Lily's uncle b the farm c the adventure playground

3 Uncle Jim wants help with ________ .
 a the adventure playground b the animals c the farm

4 The water is for ________ .
 a the hens b the horse c the goats

5 They need to feed ________ .
 a the dog b the horse c the hens

15 Read and tick the activities that show the value: take care of pets and animals.

1	☑	love	4	☐	play with	7	☐	feed
2	☐	borrow	5	☐	take for a walk	8	☐	watch TV
3	☐	give water	6	☐	do homework	9	☐	brush hair

16 Circle the words with the *cr* sound.

1

2

3

4

5
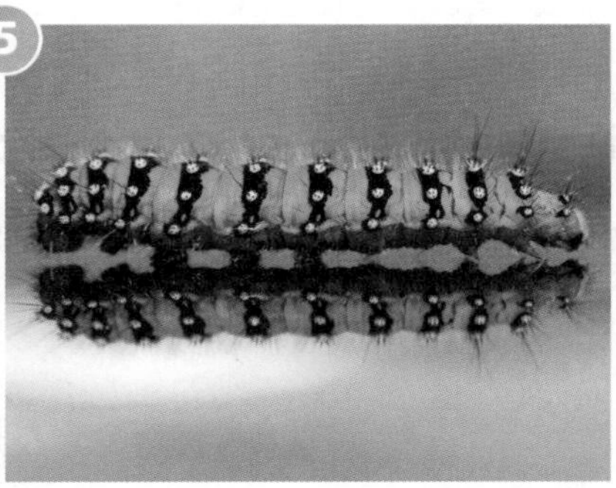

6

7

8

9

What type of work is it?

1 Match the types of work with the pictures.

a outdoor work **b** factory work **c** transport work **d** shop work

1  b

2 

3 

4 

5 

6 

2 Look and put the pictures in the correct order.

a outdoor work **b** factory work **c** transport work **d** shop work

1

 d

 ______

 ______

 ______

2

 ______

 ______

 ______

 ______

Evaluation

1 Find and circle the words. Then match.

1 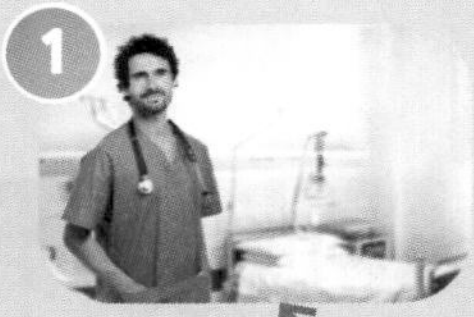
2 
3 
4 
5 

artistbusdriverbusinesswomannursebusinessmanactordoctorvetpilotsinger

6 
7 
8 
9 
10 

2 Think Look and complete the questions and answers.

1 

What does your grandfather do ?

He's a nurse . ________ he work?

He works in a ________ .

2 

________ mum ________ ?

She's an ________ . ________ she work?

She works on TV .

3 About Me Complete the sentences about this unit.

1 I can talk about ________ .

2 I can write about ________ .

3 My favourite part is ________ .

4 Puzzle Guess what it is.

This person can fly a helicopter.

Who is it? ________

Go to page 93 and write the answer.

4 Wild animals

1 Look and tick the correct words.

1
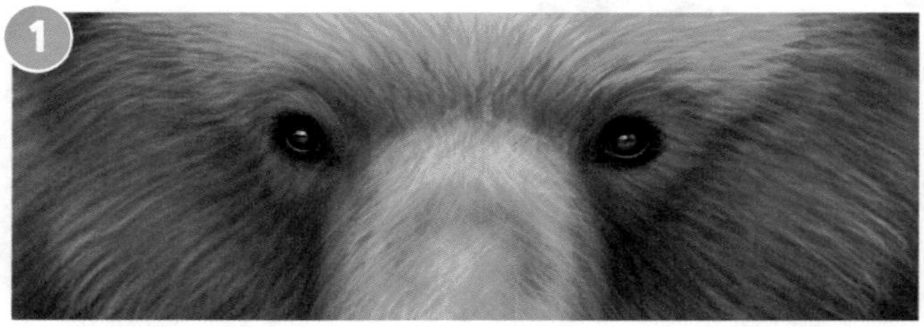

bat ☐ bear ☑

2

monkey ☐ gorilla ☐

3

parrot ☐ owl ☐

4

panda ☐ penguin ☐

5

kangaroo ☐ jaguar ☐

6
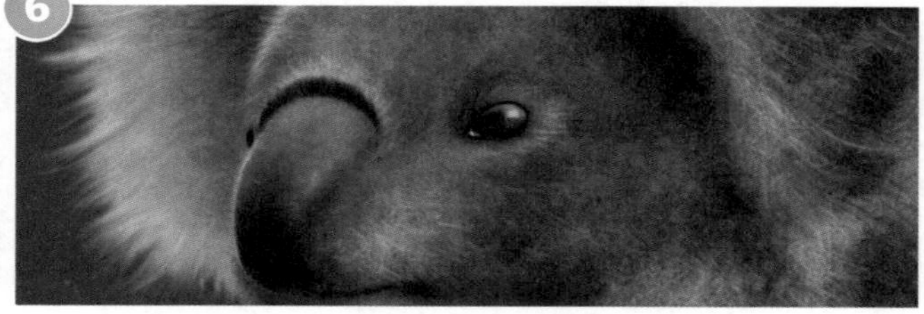

owl ☐ koala ☐

2 Write the words.

kangaroo bat penguin ~~parrot~~ panda jaguar

It can fly.	It's got a long tail.	It's black and white.
parrot	________	________
________	________	________

My picture dictionary → Go to page 88: Find and write the new words.

3 Read and choose the correct words.

1	Bears	are smaller than are bigger than	gorillas.
2	Kangaroos	are slower than are quicker than	jaguars.
3	Koalas	are noisier than are quieter than	bats.
4	Rabbits	are slower than are quicker than	penguins.
5	Parrots	are noisier than are quieter than	snails.

4 Look and complete the sentences. Use the words in the box.

1 Gorillas are *bigger* than jaguars.
2 Gorillas are ______ than koalas.
3 Koalas ______ jaguars.
4 Jaguars ______ gorillas.

big small

5 Parrots are ______ than bats.
6 Bats are ______ than butterflies.
7 Butterflies ______ bats.
8 Bats ______ parrots.

noisy quiet

5 Think Read and circle the correct words.

1	Are koalas **quicker** / **slower** (circled) than gorillas?	Yes, they are.
2	Are owls **smaller** / **bigger** than pandas?	No, they aren't.
3	Are horses **taller** / **shorter** than gorillas?	No, they aren't.
4	Are parrots **noisier** / **quieter** than guinea pigs?	Yes, they are.
5	Are cats **longer** / **shorter** than jaguars?	No, they aren't.

6 Look and use the words to complete the questions.

quick / slow

1 Are jaguars *quicker than* tortoises?
Yes, they are.

2 Are tortoises ________________ jaguars?
Yes, they are.

tall / short

3 Are kangaroos ________________ penguins?
No, they aren't.

4 Are penguins ________________ kangaroos?
No, they aren't.

long / short

5 Are dolphins ________________ caterpillars?
Yes, they are.

6 Are caterpillars ________________ dolphins?
Yes, they are.

7 About Me Complete the questions and write the answers.

~~tall~~ short quiet noisy

1 Are you *taller than* your friend? ________________

2 Are you ________________ your friend? ________________

3 ________________ your friend? ________________

4 ________________ your friend? ________________

Skills: *Writing*

8 Read the paragraph and write the words.

taller spots Africa ~~long~~ leaves

My favourite animal

My favourite animal is the giraffe. Giraffes are very tall. They are brown and white and they've got a [1] *long* neck and [2] ________ . They come from [3] ________ . They are wild animals, not pets. They eat [4] ________ . They are [5] ________ than a tree.

9 About Me Answer the questions.

1 What's your favourite animal?

____

2 What does it look like?

____

3 Where does it come from?

____

4 What does it eat?

____

5 Is it taller than a tree?

____

10 About Me Write about your favourite animal.

My favourite animal ________________________________

____

____

____

11 About Me Guess your friend's favourite animal.

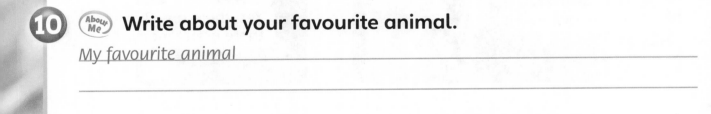

It's smaller than a cat. It's slower than a guinea pig. It eats grass.

Is it a tortoise?

Yes, it is.

12 Read and number in order.

a

Grandpa, can you make an owl box for us?
Yes – you can help.

b

It's beautiful.
There you are! A house for an owl!

c

Where are the nails?
Here they are.
Can you pass them, please?

d

No, Anna. We need bigger boxes. Owls are bigger than other birds.
Are these owl boxes?
Let's make one.

e

Thank you. It's for the nature zone.
Wow! There are lots of boxes.
It's an owl town!

f

Are there bird boxes in your garden, Tom?
Yes, there are. But there aren't many.
1

13 Look at activity 12. Answer the questions.

1 What do they want to make? An owl box.

2 Why do they need to make one? ______________________

3 Who helps them to make it? ______________________

4 What do they need to make it? ______________________

5 What's an owl box? ______________________

14 Look and tick the pictures that show the value: look after nature.

1

2

3

4

5

6

15 Look and write the words with the *fr* sound.

1 ______________

2 ______________

3 ______________

a

b

c

d

e
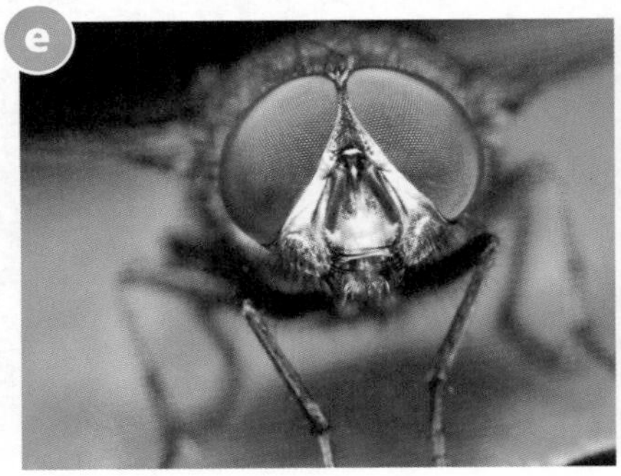

f

What animal group is it?

1 **Read the questions and write the words in the correct boxes.**

snake frog panda ~~parrot~~ | fish amphibian ~~bird~~ mammal reptile

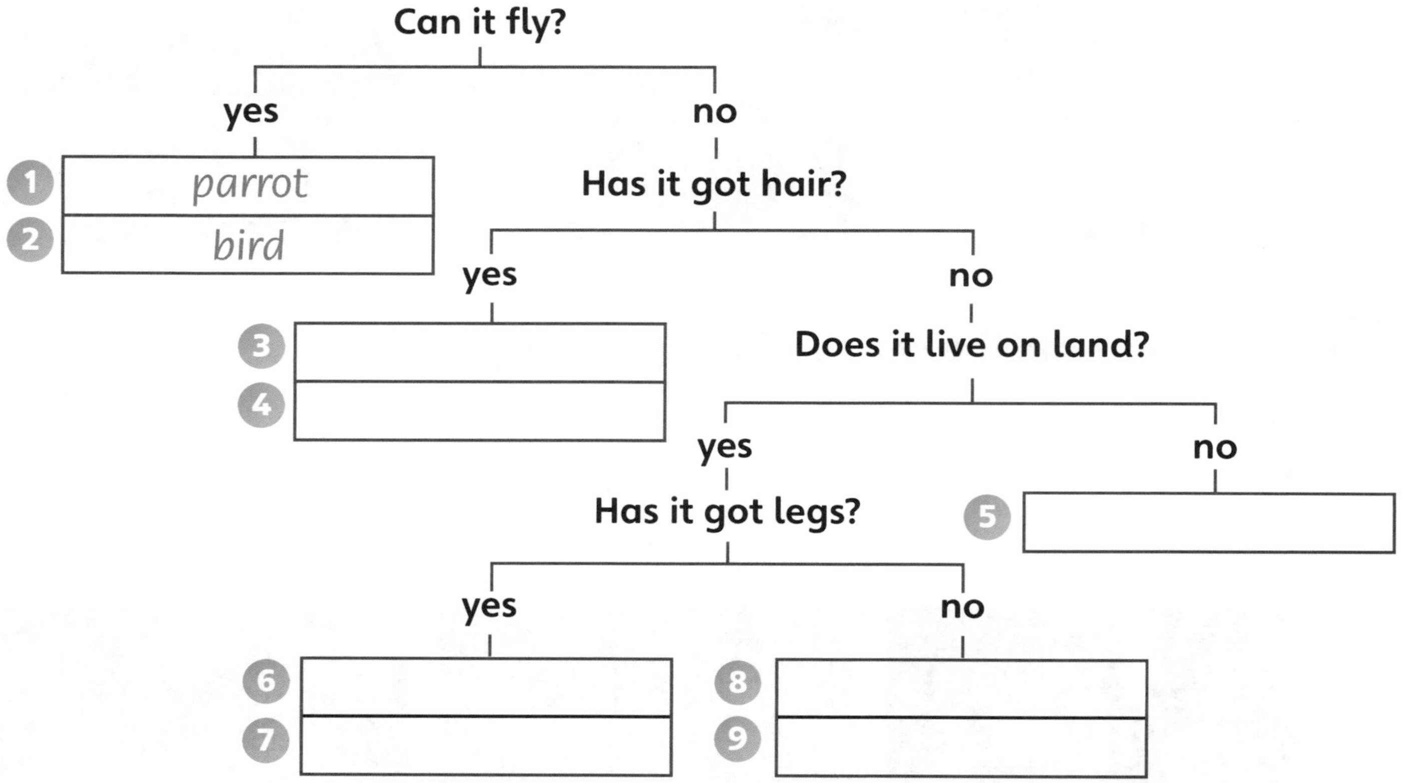

Can it fly?
yes
no
1 parrot
2 bird
Has it got hair?
yes
no
3
4
Does it live on land?
yes
no
5
Has it got legs?
yes
no
6
7
8
9

2 **Look at activity 1. Write about a reptile, a bird, a mammal and an amphibian.**

1 *A snake is a reptile. It can't fly and it hasn't got hair. It lives on land.*

2 ______

3 ______

4 ______

Evaluation

1 Think **Find and circle ten animal words→↓. Use the extra letters to answer the question.**

j	a	g	u	a	r	c	b	p	i
p	a	r	r	o	t	f	e	a	k
g	o	r	i	l	l	a	a	n	o
o	w	l	b	a	t	a	r	d	a
p	e	n	g	u	i	n	r	a	l
a	k	a	n	g	a	r	o	o	a

Where do gorillas come from?
A_ _ _ _ _

2 **Look and complete the sentences.**

~~big~~ small quiet quick

1 Gorillas are *bigger* than koalas.

2 Owls are ______ than parrots.

3 Bats ______ kangaroos.

4 Jaguars ______ penguins.

3 About Me **Complete the sentences about this unit.**

1 I can talk about ______ .

2 I can write about ______ .

3 My favourite part is ______ .

4 Puzzle **Guess what it is.**

It's big and black and white. It eats leaves. What is it? ______

Go to page 93 and write the answer.

Review Units 3 and 4

1 Look and tick the correct answers.

1
146
58
2
3
4

1 What do you want to be?

- [✓] a I want to be a teacher.
- [ ] b I want to be a businessman.

2 Do you want to be a singer?

- [ ] a Yes, I do.
- [ ] b No, I don't. I want to be a farmer.

3 Do you want to be a footballer?

- [ ] a Yes, I do.
- [ ] b No, I don't. I want to be a bus driver.

4 What do you want to be?

- [ ] a I want to be an actor.
- [ ] b I want to be a businesswoman.

2 Read and complete the conversation.

Paul
Gemma

Gemma: _What does your_ mum __________ ?

Paul: She's an __________ .
She likes drawing and painting.

Gemma: __________ she
__________ ?

Paul: She works in a studio.

Gemma: Do you __________ an artist too?

Paul: No, I don't. I like Maths.
I __________ a teacher.

3 Think Look and write the questions and answers.

short long small ~~big~~

wallaby
kangaroo

bear
squirrel monkey

1 Are kangaroos *bigger than* wallabies? Yes, they are.
2 Are wallabies ______________ kangaroos? Yes, ______________ .
3 Are squirrel monkey tails ______________ bear tails? No, ______________ .
4 Are bear tails ______________ squirrel monkey tails? No, ______________ .

4 About Me Use the words to complete the questions. Then write answers.

~~small~~ noisy quick big fast

1 Are you *smaller than* a gorilla? *Yes, I am.*
2 Are you ______________ a parrot? ______________
3 Are you ______________ a jaguar? ______________
4 Are you ______________ a koala? ______________
5 Are you ______________ a tortoise? ______________

5 Food and drink

1 Look and write the words.

1 

pous

soup

2 

ladsa

3 

zipza

4 

satap

5 

turgoyh

6 

sispcr

7 

tuicisb

8 

tuns

9 

eat

10 

eofefc

2 Think What do they want for lunch? Read and then write the words.

Tim: I want pizza for lunch!

Gina: I don't. I want pasta and salad.

Tim: I want salad, too. And yoghurt. I like yoghurt.

Gina: I want tea and a biscuit, too.

Tim: I want tea, too.

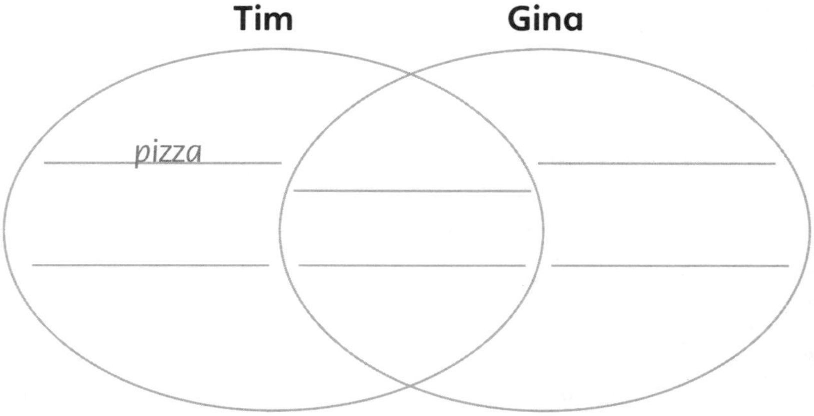
Tim
Gina
pizza

My picture dictionary → Go to page 89: Find and write the new words.

3 Look and count. Then complete the sentences.

0	1–2	3–4	5–6
never	sometimes	usually	always

1 I ___usually___ have tea for lunch.

2 I __________ have milk for lunch

3 I __________ have fish for dinner.

4 I __________ have coffee for breakfast.

5 I __________ have apples for breakfast.

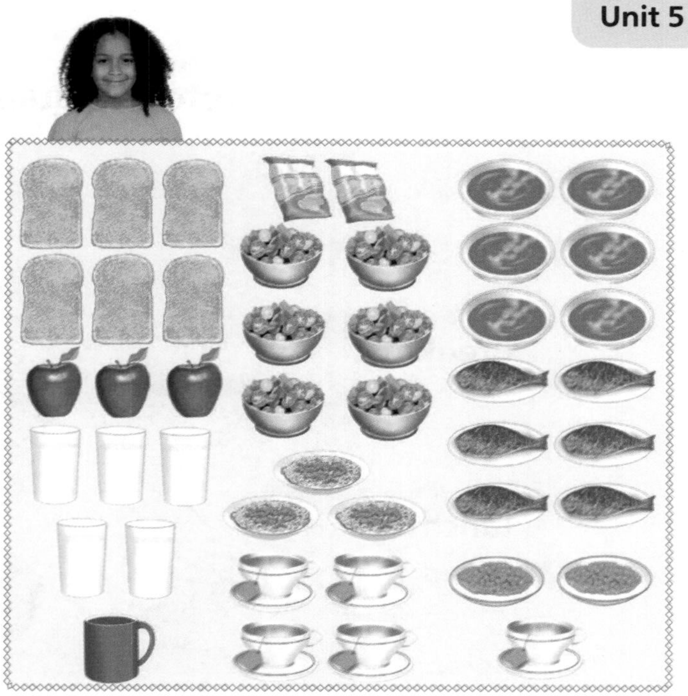

breakfast lunch dinner

4 Look at activity 3. Then complete the sentences.

1  She ___always has toast___ for breakfast.

2  She __________ for lunch.

3  She __________ for dinner.

4 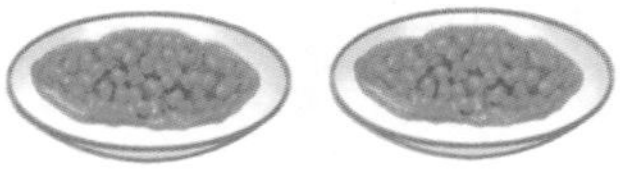 She __________ for dinner.

5  She __________ for breakfast.

5 About Me Complete the sentences.

1 I __________ for breakfast.

2 I __________ for lunch.

3 I __________ for dinner.

6 Look and complete the questions and answers.

	Mia 		
breakfast	✓✓✓ 	✓ 	✓✓ 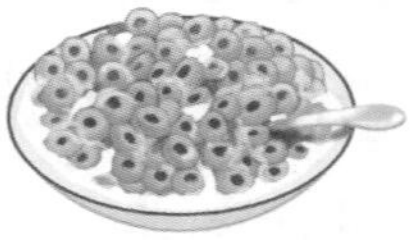
lunch	✓ 	✓✓✓ 	✓✓ 
dinner	✓✓ 	✓✓✓ 	✓ 

	never
✓	sometimes
✓✓	usually
✓✓✓	every day

1 ___How often do you have___ cereal for breakfast?

I ___usually___ have cereal for breakfast.

2 ____________________ salad for lunch?

I have salad for lunch ____________ .

3 ____________________ meat for dinner?

I ____________ meat for dinner ____________ .

4 ____________________ carrots for dinner?

____

5 ____________________ yoghurt for breakfast?

____

7 About Me Answer the questions.

1 How often do you have cereal for breakfast? ____________

2 How often do you have salad for lunch? ____________

3 How often do you have fish for dinner? ____________

Skills: *Writing*

8 About Me **Make a lunch diary. Write what you eat and drink for lunch every day.**

biscuits coffee crisps nuts pasta pizza salad soup tea yoghurt

Monday	Tuesday	Wednesday	Thursday	Friday

9 About Me **Look at activity 8. Answer the questions.**

1 What do you usually have for lunch? ______

2 What do you sometimes have for lunch? ______

3 What do you eat or drink every day for lunch? ______

4 What do you never have for lunch? ______

5 Do you have a healthy lunch? ______

10 About Me **Write about what you eat for lunch.**

I usually eat ______

______

______

______

______

11 About Me **Ask and answer with a friend.**

What do you eat for lunch?

I usually have rice and beans. Sometimes I drink milk.

12 Read and match.

1 Can I have two, please?
2 ~~£15! That's a lot of money.~~
3 Let's wash our hands first.
4 How about selling fruit?

a

How can we get £15?
2
Week 5
We need bean bags.
£15

b

I can give you £10 to buy the fruit.
Thanks, Dad!

c

Good idea. Come on, Anna.
OK.

d

How much is the fruit salad?
It's one pound.
£1
Yes, of course. Here you are.

13 Look at activity 12. Write *yes* or *no*.

1 They need to get a lot of money. *yes*
2 Lucas's dad gives them money to buy fruit. ______
3 Washing your hands before touching food is a good idea. ______
4 The fruit salad costs two pounds. ______
5 Lucas's grandma sells fruit salad. ______

14 Look and tick the pictures that show the value: be clean around food.

1

a

b

2

a

b

3

a

b
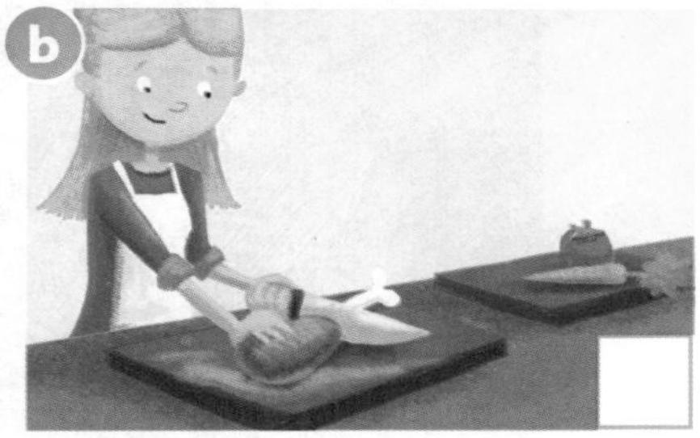

15 Circle the words with the *ar* sound.

1

2

3

4

5

6

7

8
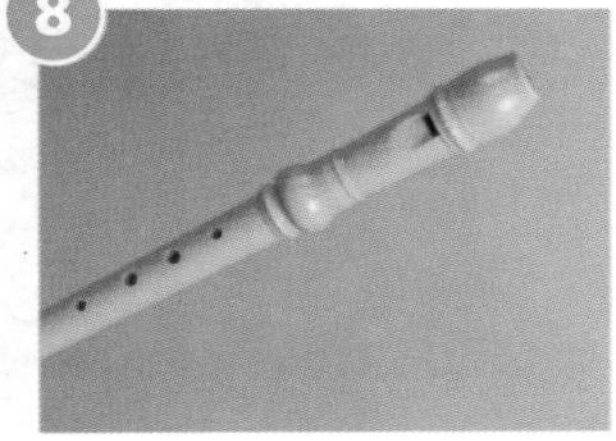

9

10

11

Where does water come from?

1 Look and write.

~~cloud~~ glacier mountain rain river sea spring well

1 cloud
2
3
4
5
6
7
8

2 Complete the sentences about water.

1 Water comes from c*louds*______ and r__________ .

2 Some people drink water from a w__________ or a s__________ .

3 We can see a g__________ in the mountains.

4 A r__________ goes to the s__________ .

Evaluation

1 Look and match.

1 yoghurt [h] 6 crisps [ ]
2 pasta [ ] 7 salad [ ]
3 tea [ ] 8 coffee [ ]
4 nuts [ ] 9 pizza [ ]
5 soup [ ] 10 biscuit [ ]

a

b
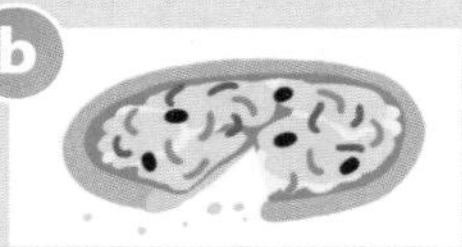
c
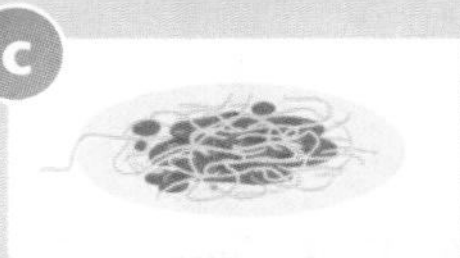
d

e

f

g

h

i

j

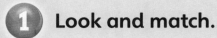

2 Look and write.

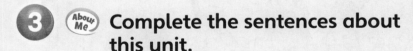

Emile	Monday	Tuesday	Wednesday	Thursday	Friday
	cake	cake	crisps	cake	cake
	nuts	nuts	cake	nuts	coffee

1 How often does Emile have crisps? *Sometimes.*
2 How often does he have cake? ____
3 How often does he have pizza? ____
4 How often does he have nuts? ____
5 How often does he have coffee? ____

3 About Me Complete the sentences about this unit.

1 I can talk about ____.
2 I can write about ____.
3 My favourite part is ____.

4 Puzzle Guess what it is.

It's a drink. It's dark brown. It's usually hot. It's not tea. What is it?

____

Go to page 93 and write the answer.

6 Health matters

1 Look and write the words.

backache
cold
cough
earache
headache
~~sore throat~~
stomachache
temperature
toothache

1 
sore throat

2 
____

3 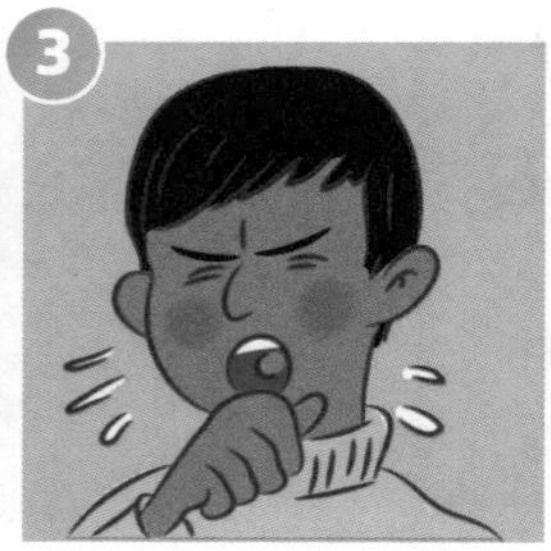
____

4 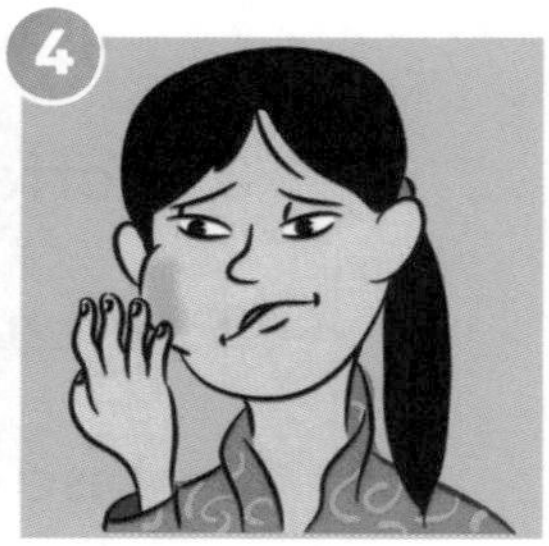
____

5 
____

6 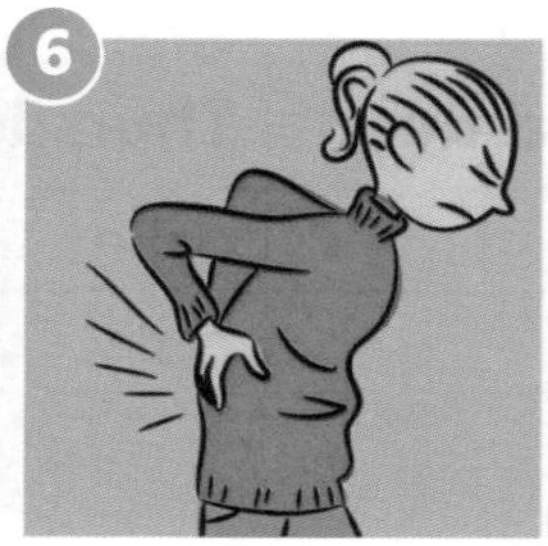
____

7 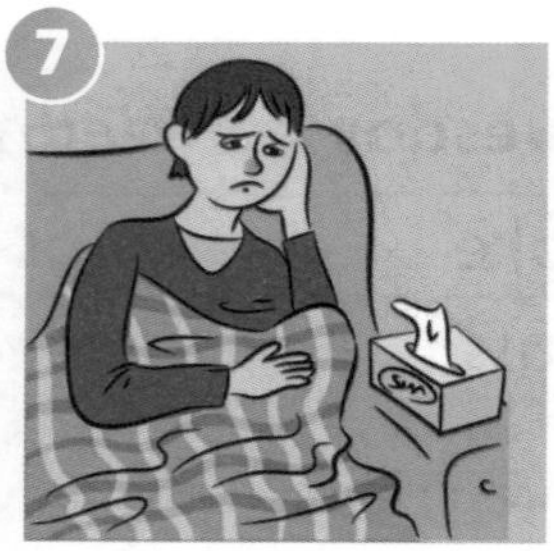
____

8 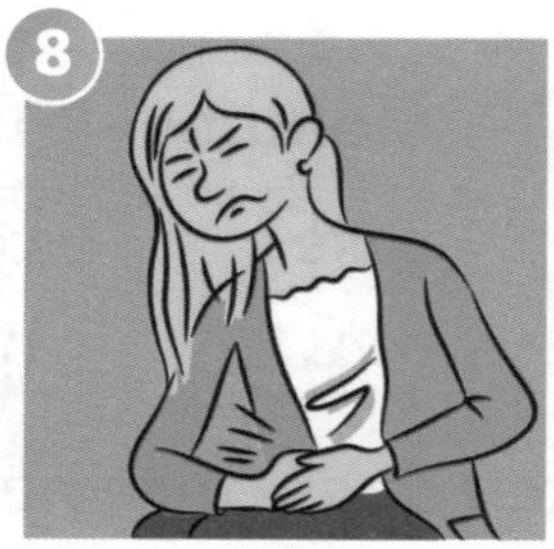
____

9 
____

2 Look and complete the sentences.

1 Dan's got a stomachache .
2 Grace's got a __________ .
3 Ann's got a __________ .
4 May's got a __________ .
5 Tony's got a __________ .

DOC
Ann
Tony
Grace
May
Dan

My picture dictionary → Go to page 90: Find and write the new words.

3 Look and write.

1 

What's the matter, Kelly?

I've got a cold, an earache and a ______.

2 

What's the ______, Bill?

I've got a ______, a ______ ______ and a ______.

3 

______, Sue?

I've got an ______, a ______ and a ______.

4 Think Look at activity 3. Write the words.

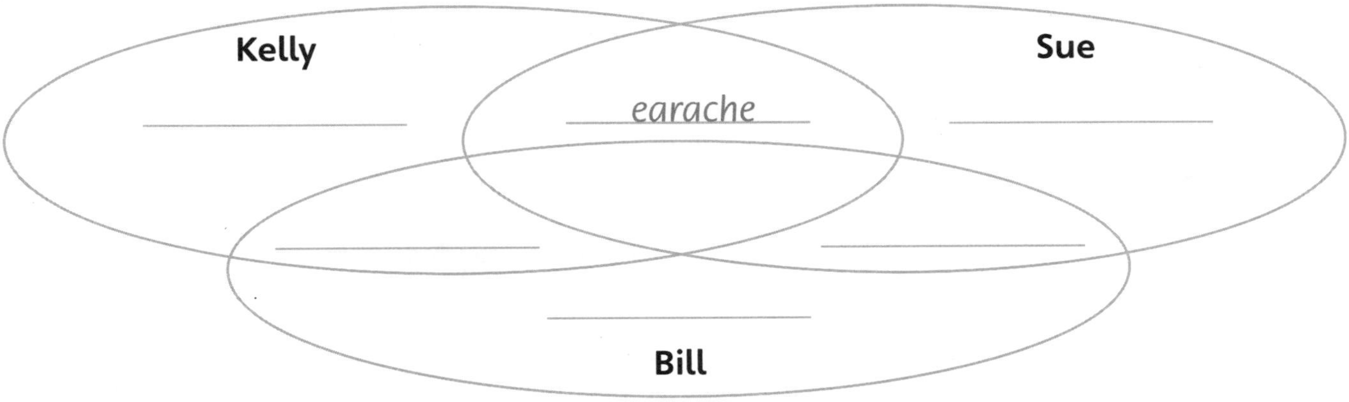
Kelly
Sue
earache
Bill

5 Look and write the questions and answers.

1 What's the matter?

I've got an earache.

2 What's the ______?

I've got ______.

3 What's the ______?

I've got ______.

4 ______?

______

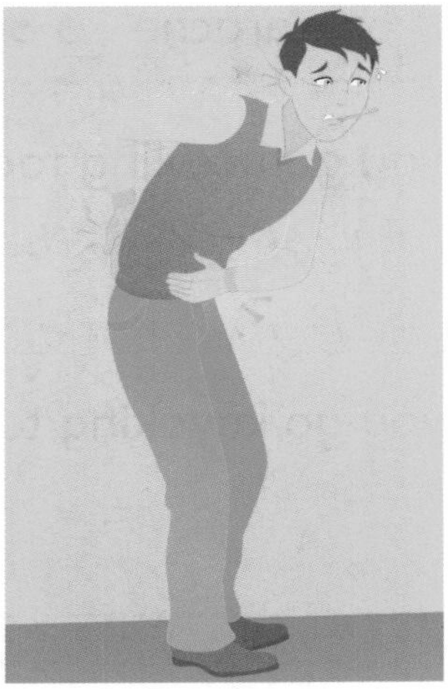

6 Complete the questions and say why you can't.

1

Can you go kayaking today?

No, I can't . I've got a temperature .

2

__________ go snowboarding today?

No, I __________ . I've got a __________ .

3

__________ go to the museum today?

____

4

__________ play football today?

____

5

__________ go swimming today?

____

7 Complete the sentences. Use the words in the box.

a cold | an earache | ~~a backache~~ | a temperature

1 Can you go bowling today?

No, I can't .

I've got a backache .

2 Can you go kayaking today?

No, __________ .

__________ .

3 Can you go to the cinema tonight?

No, __________ .

__________ .

4 Can you go swimming tomorrow?

No, __________ .

__________ .

Skills: *Writing*

8 Read the paragraph and write the words.

~~favourite~~ wash yoghurt lunch need

Apple and nut salad is my [1] *favourite* salad. It's healthy because apples and nuts are good for you. I sometimes have this salad for [2] ________ .

- You [3] ________ apples, nuts, cheese, yoghurt and carrots.
- [4] ________ the fruit and vegetables. Cut the apples, carrots and cheese.
- Add some [5] ________ .

9 About Me Answer the questions.

1 What's your favourite healthy food or drink?

____

2 Why is it healthy?

____

3 What do you need?

____

4 How do you make it?

____

5 How often do you eat/drink it?

____

10 About Me Write a recipe for your favourite healthy food or drink.

____

____

____

____

11 About Me Ask and answer with a friend.

What's your favourite healthy food or drink?

My favourite healthy food is salad.

12 Read and write the words.

headache ~~competition~~ leg hurts very good OK now

a
competition
today
Win a skateboard!
It's a competition!
Go, Chris!
b
Oh dear!
Are you OK, Chris?
Yes, I think so. My ________, but I'm OK. Don't worry.
c
Have you got a ________, Chris?
No, I'm ________.
But where's your skateboard?
d
Well done, Max!
Sorry, Chris!
1
That's OK! I'm good at skateboarding, but Max is ________!

13 Look at activity 12. Circle the correct words.

1 Chris has a skateboarding **club** / **competition** / **team**.
2 Chris's **leg** / **head** / **ear** hurts.
3 Chris says he hasn't got a **backache** / **stomachache** / **headache**.
4 Max is **really bad** / **OK** / **really good** at skateboarding.
5 **Chris** / **Tom** / **Lily** is a good sport.

14 Look and tick the pictures that show the value: be a good sport.

1

Good game.
✓

2

I'm number 1!

3

You're not very good.
Wah!

4

Well done!

15 Connect the words with the *sp* sound.

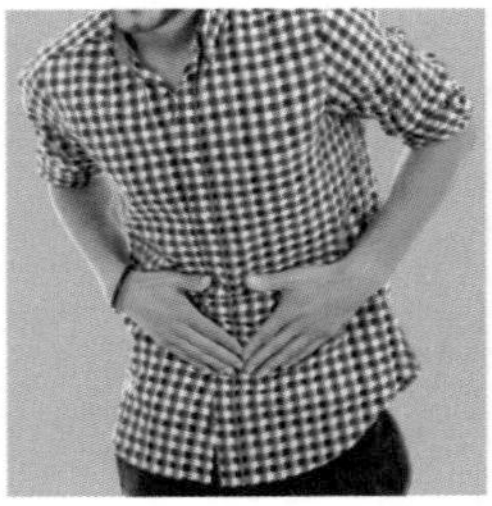

A B C
apple book cat

What can we use plants for?

1 Read and match.

1 We can use trees for fuel. c
2 We can use plants to give us cereal. ____
3 We can use the fruit from plants for medicine. ____
4 We can use the wood from trees to give us shelter. ____
5 We can use plants to make fabric. ____

a

b

c

d

e

2 Draw a plant. Then write three ways we can use your plant.

1 ______________________________
____
____

2 ______________________________
____
____

3 ______________________________
____
____

Evaluation

1 Think Look and then complete the sentences.

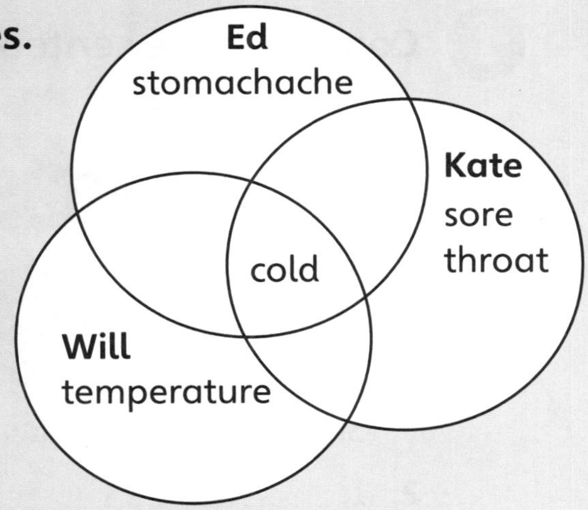
Ed
stomachache
Kate
sore
throat
cold
Will
temperature

1 ___What's the matter___ with Will?
He's got a ___cold___ and
a ______ .

2 ______ Ed?
He's got a ______ and
a ______ .

3 ______ Kate?
______ and
a ______ .

2 Read and then complete the answers.

1 Can you go to the cinema today?
(My head hurts.)
No, I ___can't___ . I've got a ___headache___ .

2 Can you go to the café tonight?
(My tooth hurts.)
No, I ______ . I've got a ______ .

3 Can you play basketball this afternoon?
(My back hurts.)
______

3 About Me Complete the sentences about this unit.

1 I can talk about ______ .
2 I can write about ______ .
3 My favourite part is ______ .

4 Puzzle Guess what it is.

Eating a lot of food can give you a ______ . What is it?

Go to page 93 and write the answer.

Review Units 5 and 6

1 Complete the sentences.

breakfast / me

lunch / Kim

✗
✓
✓✓
✓
✓
✓✓✓

✗ = never
✓ = sometimes
✓✓ = usually
✓✓✓ = always

1 She *sometimes has* soup for lunch.
2 I ______________________ yoghurt for breakfast.
3 She ______________________ rice for lunch.
4 I ______________________ tea for breakfast.
5 She ______________________ a sandwich for lunch.
6 I ______________________ toast for breakfast.

2 Think Read and then write the words.

Leo and Carol usually have pizza for lunch and Billy usually has fish. Sometimes Leo has a sandwich and sometimes Billy and Carol have salad. Leo and Billy usually have crisps and Carol usually has yoghurt. Carol, Billy and Leo always drink tea for lunch.

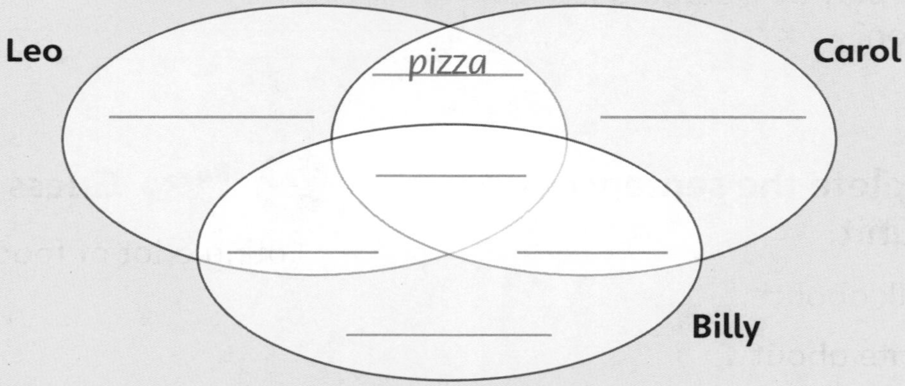
Leo
pizza
Carol
Billy

3 About Me Answer the questions.

1 What do you always have for breakfast? ______________________
2 What do you usually have for lunch? ______________________
3 What do you sometimes have for dinner? ______________________
4 What do you never have for dinner? ______________________

4 Think Find the letters and write the words. Then match.

a	b	c	d	e	f	g	h	i	j	k	l	m
■	▼	◆	✖	●	✚	★	◗	▮	⁚	↓	♥	✱
n	**o**	**p**	**q**	**r**	**s**	**t**	**u**	**v**	**w**	**x**	**y**	**z**
()	◠	⬢	◖	▲	▰	▬	↑	✿	Ɛ	◂▸	⬮	ϟ

1 ◆ ◠ ↑ ★ ◗
c o u g h

2 ◗ ● ■ ✖ ■ ◆ ◗ ●
_ _ _ _ _ _ _ _

3 ▬ ● ✱ ⬢ ● ▲ ■ ▬ ↑ ▲ ●
_ _ _ _ _ _ _ _ _ _ _

4 ▬ ◠ ◠ ▬ ◗ ■ ◆ ◗ ●
_ _ _ _ _ _ _ _ _

5 ◆ ◠ ♥ ✖
_ _ _ _

6 ▰ ◠ ▲ ●   ▬ ◗ ▲ ◠ ■ ▬
_ _ _ _   _ _ _ _ _ _

7 ▼ ■ ◆ ↓ ■ ◆ ◗ ●
_ _ _ _ _ _ _ _

8 ▰ ▬ ◠ ✱ ■ ◆ ◗ ■ ◆ ◗ ●
_ _ _ _ _ _ _ _ _ _ _

9 ● ■ ▲ ■ ◆ ◗ ●
_ _ _ _ _ _ _

a  ☐

b  ☐

c  ☐

d  ☐

e  ☐

f  1

g  ☐

h  ☐

i  ☐

5 Read and complete the answers.

Oh dear ~~I think so~~ I don't think so Oh, good Don't worry

1 Are you OK?
Yes, I think so .
__________ .
__________ !

2 Are you OK?
No, __________ . I've got an earache.
__________ !

7 Buildings

1 Look and number.

1 ~~attic~~
2 basement
3 stairs
4 lift
5 roof
6 ground floor
7 first floor
8 second floor
9 third floor
10 garage

1

2 Look at activity 1. Write the words.

1 There's a kite on the ___roof___ .
2 There's a cat in the ______________ .
3 There's a car in the ______________ .
4 There's a skateboard on the ______________ .
5 There's a man on the ______________ ______________ .
6 There's a woman on the ______________ ______________ .

My picture dictionary → Go to page 91: Find and write the new words.

3 Put the words in order. Then write the number.

1

1 you / Where / morning / yesterday / were / ?

Where were you yesterday morning?

the / was / I / kitchen / in / .

I was in the kitchen.

2 were / afternoon / you / Where / yesterday / ?

second / on / I / the / was / floor / .

3 yesterday / you / evening / were / Where / ?

in / I / room / the / was / living / .

4 morning / were / yesterday / Where / you / ?

was / I / in / garage / the / .

5 night / were / you / last / Where / ?

bedroom / floor / I / in / my / on / the / third / was / .

4 About Me Answer the questions.

1 Where were you yesterday morning?

2 Where were you yesterday afternoon?

3 Where were you yesterday evening?

4 Where were you last night?

5 Think Look and tick *Yes, I was* or *No, I wasn't*.

	Yes, I was.	No, I wasn't.
1 Were you at the sports field yesterday morning?	☐	✓
2 Were you at the beach yesterday morning?	☐	☐
3 Were you at a restaurant yesterday afternoon?	☐	☐
4 Were you at home last night?	☐	☐
5 Were you at the cinema yesterday evening?	☐	☐

10 o'clock at the beach
3 o'clock at the shopping centre
6 o'clock at the sports field
11 o'clock at home

6 Look and write.

yesterday morning	yesterday afternoon	yesterday evening	last night

1 *Were you* at the sports centre yesterday evening? Yes, *I was*.

2 ______ at home yesterday afternoon? No, ______.

3 ______ at school yesterday afternoon? Yes, ______.

4 ______ in your bedroom yesterday morning? Yes, ______.

5 ______ at the cinema last night? No, ______.

7 About Me Answer the questions.

1 Were you at school yesterday morning? ______

2 Were you at the library yesterday afternoon? ______

3 Were you on the bus yesterday evening? ______

4 Were you at a restaurant last night? ______

Skills: *Writing*

8 **Read the text. Circle the answers to the questions.**

On Saturday morning, I was at the park with my dog. Then I was at a café at lunchtime. In the afternoon, I was at the sports centre. It was exciting. I love playing basketball! In the evening, I was at the cinema.

1 Where were you in the morning?
2 Where were you at lunchtime?
3 Where were you in the afternoon?
4 Where were you in the evening?

9 About Me **Look at activity 8. Choose a day. Answer the questions for you.**

Day: ______________________

1 ____
2 ____
3 ____
4 ____

10 About Me **Write about your day.**

____
____
____
____
____
____
____
____

11 About Me **Ask and answer with a friend.**

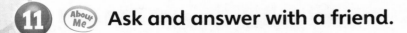

Where were you in the morning?

I was at school.

12 Read and number in order.

a

No! It's a tortoise!
It looks like my cousin Kim's tortoise!
Let's call and ask her.

b

Oh, Speedy! Thank you so much!
What can we give you for a reward?
LOST TORTOIS REWAR

c

Hello. I think we've got your tortoise.
Great! Where was he?
He was in my garage!

d

Here's my old bike. Oh dear!
Look. Is that a helmet?
1

e

Have you got an old bike?
Yes, I have!
A helmet too, please!

f

Hello?
Hello. It's Lily. Is Kim there, please?
Yes, she is. Just a minute.

13 Look at activity 12. Answer the questions.

1 Who has an old bike? Lily
2 Is it a helmet or a tortoise? ____________
3 Whose tortoise is it? ____________
4 Where was the tortoise? ____________
5 What's the tortoise's name? ____________

14 Look and tick the pictures that show the value: look after your possessions.

1

2

3

4

5

6

15 Colour the words with the letters *ck*.

1
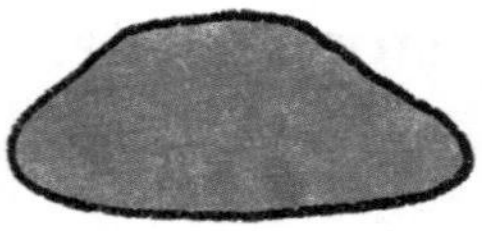

2

3

4
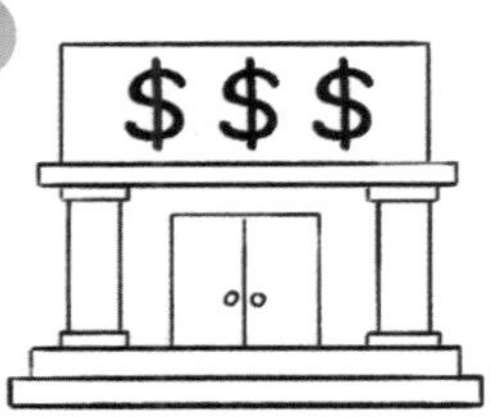
$ $ $

5

6

7

8

What materials were buildings made of?

1 Look and match.

1

2
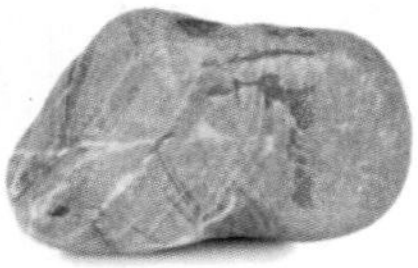

3

4
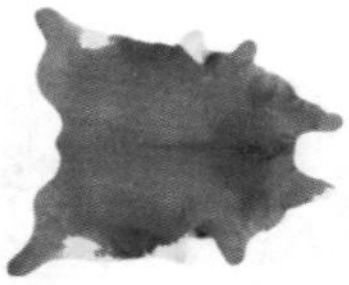

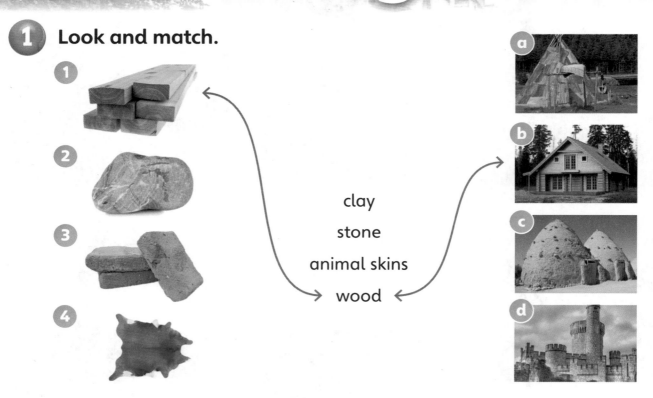

clay
stone
animal skins
wood

a

b

c

d

2 Draw your house. Then write about the old building and your house.

1 The old building was made of _stone_ . My house is made of ____________ .

2 The old building is ____________ than my house.

3 The old building has got ____________ floors. My house has got ____________ floors.

4 I don't think the old building has got a ____________ .

5 My house has got a ____________ .

Old stone castle.

My house.

Evaluation

1 Think Do the word puzzle.

Across →

1 You can put a car and a bicycle here.
3 It's below the third floor.
5 It's between the second floor and the attic.
7 It's below the ground floor.
8 It's above the ground floor.

Down ↓

2 It's where you usually come in the house.
4 It's above the third floor and below the roof.
6 It's above the attic.

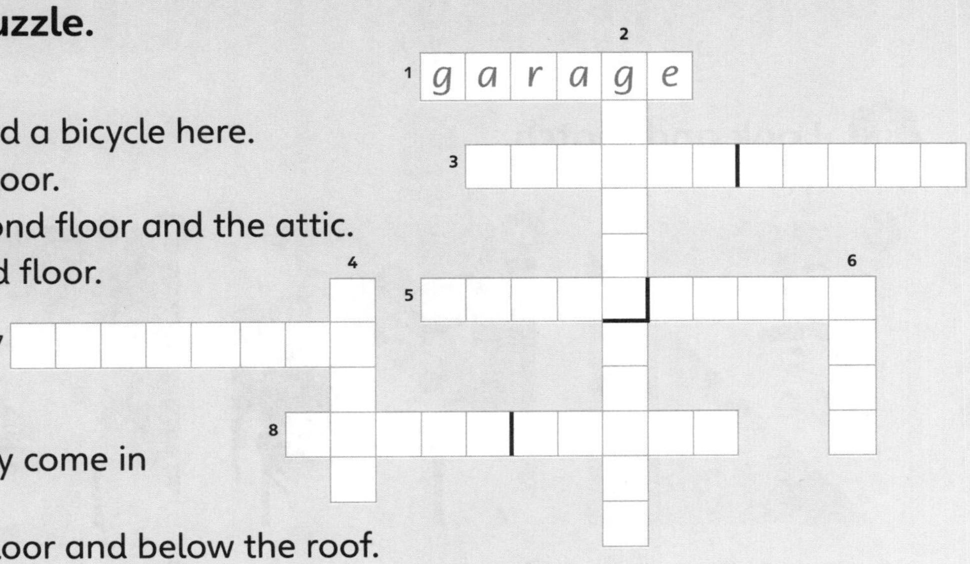
1 garage
2
3
4
5
6
7
8

2 Complete the questions and answers.

1 **Mark:** Where ___*were you*___ yesterday morning?
2 **Eva:** ________________ at the beach.
3 **Mark:** Where were you in the afternoon?
4 **Eva:** ________________ at the cinema.
5 **Mark:** ________________ at a restaurant in the evening?
6 **Eva:** No, ________________ . I was at home.

I was
I wasn't
~~were you~~
Were you
I was

3 About Me Complete the sentences about this unit.

1 I can talk about ________________ .
2 I can write about ________________ .
3 My favourite part is ________________ .

4 Puzzle Guess what it is.

It's quicker than the stairs.
What is it? ________________

Go to page 93 and write the answer.

8 Weather

1 Look and match.

a
b

1 snowy [a]

a
b

2 cloudy [ ]

a
b

3 windy [ ]

a
b

4 sunny [ ]

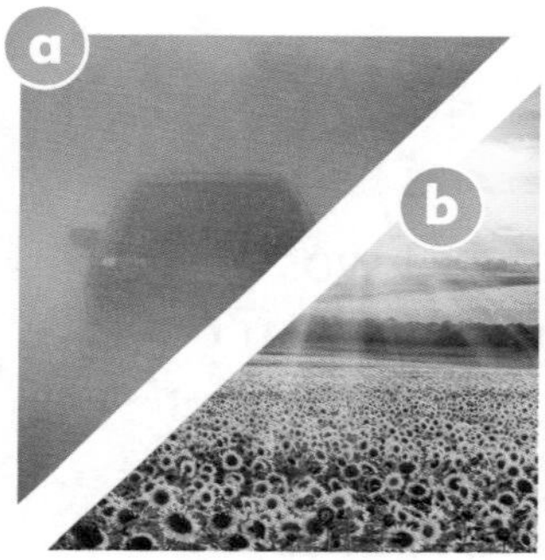

a
b

5 foggy [ ]

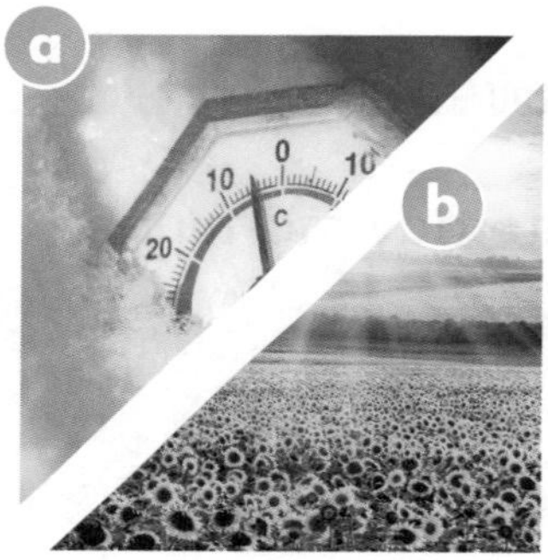

a
b

6 cold [ ]

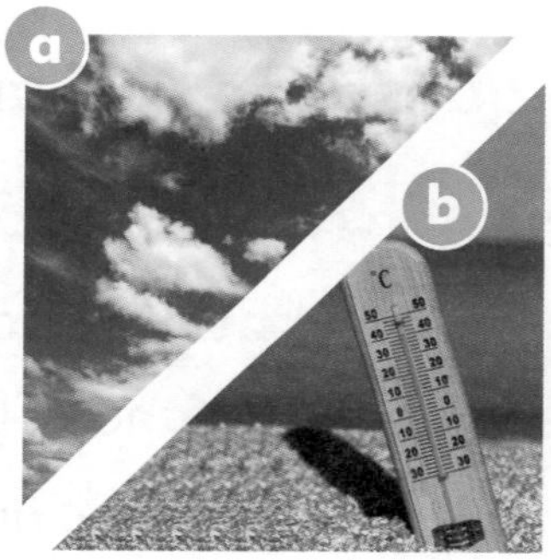

a
b

7 hot [ ]

a
b

8 rainy [ ]

2 Write the words.

~~cold~~ hot warm

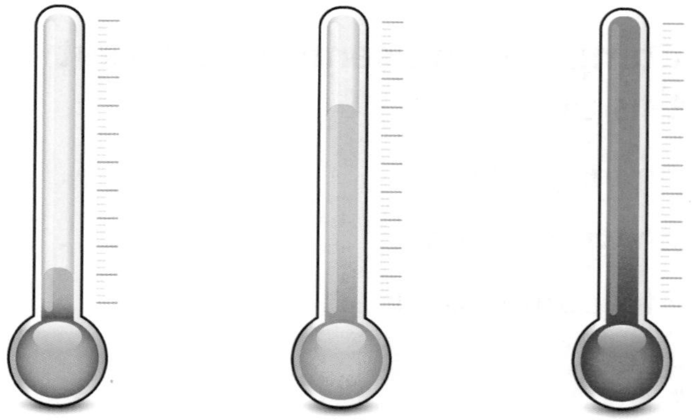

1 cold 2 ________ 3 ________

My picture dictionary → Go to page 92: Find and write the new words.

3 Look and write.

Yesterday at 10:00.

What was the weather like yesterday morning?

It was warm and rainy.

Yesterday at 15:00.

__________ the weather like ________________ ?

__________ and __________ .

Yesterday at 19:00.

__________ the weather like ________________ ?

____

Yesterday at 23:00.

__________ the weather like ________________ ?

__________ and __________ .

Today.

____ ?

____

4 About Me Answer the questions.

1 What was the weather like yesterday morning?

____

2 What was the weather like last night?

____

3 What's the weather like today?

____

4 What's your favourite weather?

____

5 Think Read and match. Then write the days.

1 Was it cold and foggy on Tuesday?
No, it wasn't. It was warm and windy.

2 Was it hot and rainy on Thursday?
No, it wasn't. It was cold and snowy.

3 Was it hot and sunny on Friday?
Yes, it was.

4 Was it cold and cloudy on Wednesday?
No, it wasn't. It was hot and rainy.

5 Was it hot and cloudy on Monday?
No, it wasn't. It was cold and cloudy.

a 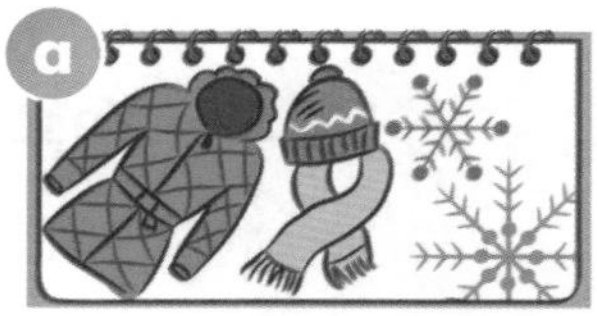 ____________

b 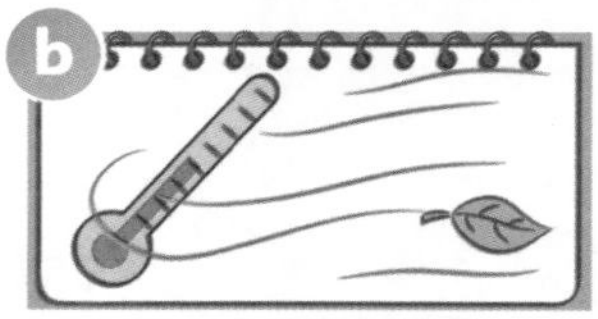 Tuesday

c  ____________

d  ____________

e  ____________

6 Look and complete the questions and answers.

1 
Tuesday

2 
Thursday

3 
Saturday

4 
Sunday

1 Was it warm and rainy on Tuesday?
Yes, it was.

2 ____________ cold and snowy on Thursday?
____

3 ____________ hot and windy on Saturday?
No, it wasn't. It was ____________ and ____________ .

4 ____________ cold and cloudy on Sunday?
____

Skills: *Writing*

7 Read about Jane's favourite festival and answer the questions.

On Sunday I was at the Bristol hot-air balloon festival with my family. The balloon festival is every August. The weather's usually hot and sunny. The festival's really big and there are lots of beautiful hot-air balloons. You can fly in a hot-air balloon. I like taking photos of the balloons. They're fantastic!

1 What's Jane's favourite festival?

____

2 When is it?

____

3 What's the weather like?

____

4 What can you see there?

____

5 What can you do at the festival?

____

8 Answer the questions for you.

1 ______________________________
2 ______________________________
3 ______________________________
4 ______________________________
5 ______________________________

9 About Me Write about your favourite festival.

____
____
____
____

10 About Me Ask and answer with a friend.

What's your favourite festival?

The Songkran water festival.

11 Read and match.

1 thank you for your hard work!
2 What time does the party start?
3 ~~Please come to the opening party on Saturday at four o'clock.~~
4 The adventure playground is now open!

a
adventure playground
Adventure Playground
Well done, everyone!
Our adventure playground is ready!
3
b
It's Saturday today!
_____
At four o'clock.
Hurry up, we're late!
c
Adventure Playground
Welcome, everyone, and _____
I want to be on TV!
d
_____

12 Look at activity 11. Write *yes* or *no*.

1 The adventure playground is ready. yes
2 The party's on Sunday. _____
3 The party starts at five o'clock. _____
4 Tom says thank you. _____
5 Anna wants to be on TV. _____

13 Look and tick the pictures that show the value: work hard and try your best.

1

2

✓

3

4

5

6

14 Look and write the words with the *nd* sound.

1 *underground station*

2 ____________________

3 ____________________

4 ____________________

5 ____________________

What's the weather like around the world?

1 Think **Put the letters in order. Then match and write.**

1 There's a **rizlbazd** with lots of snow. [e] blizzard

2 It's very cloudy and there's a **rsairtnmo**. [ ] ________

3 There's a **uihrrance** above the sea. [ ] ________

4 There's a **rnootda**. It looks like a cone. [ ] ________

5 There's **hteundr** and **ghnlintig**. [ ] ________ and ________

a

b

c

d

e

2 **What's the weather like in Adventure Land? Draw and write.**

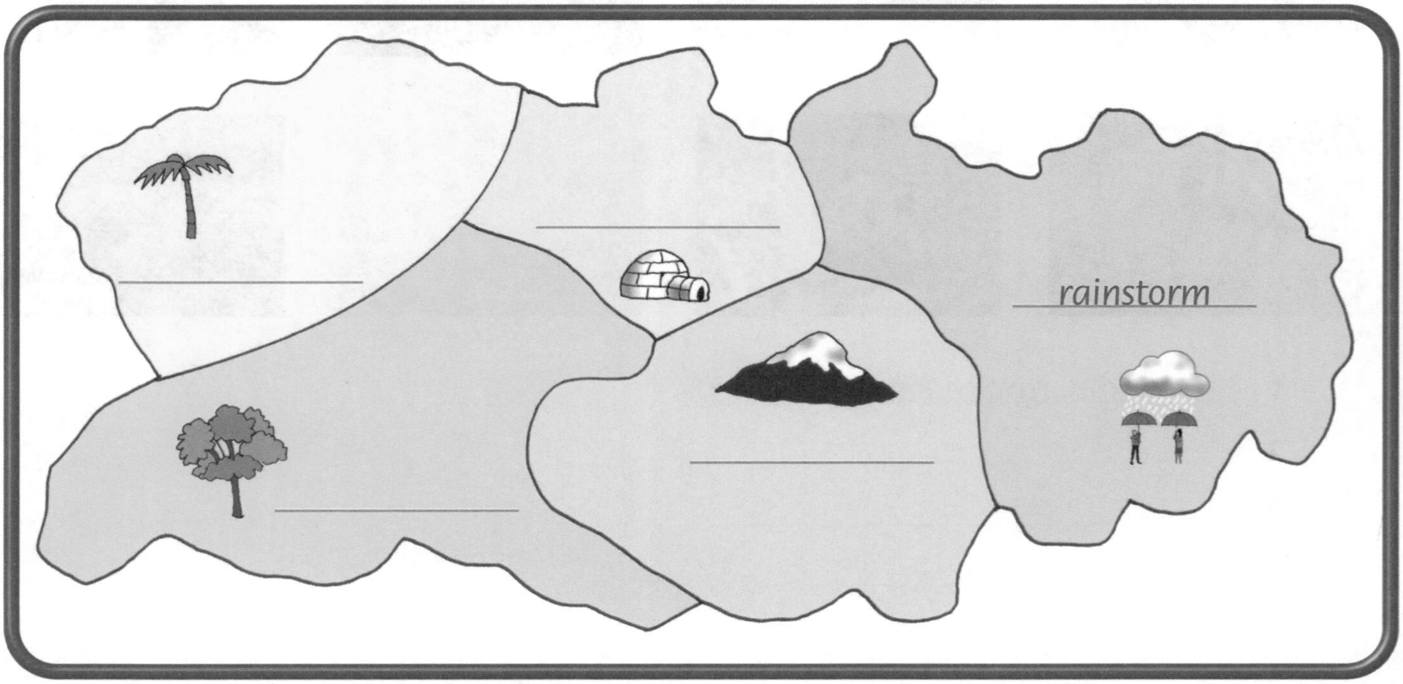
rainstorm

Evaluation

1 Look and write.

yesterday morning	yesterday afternoon	yesterday evening	last night

it was
it was
It was
it wasn't
Was it
Was it
~~What was~~
yesterday evening
~~yesterday morning~~
yesterday afternoon
Was it

1 *What was* the weather like *yesterday morning* ?
______ cold and foggy.

2 ______ warm and windy last night?
No, ______ . It was cold and snowy.

3 ______ warm and windy ______ ? Yes, ______ .

4 ______ cold and rainy ______ ? Yes, ______ .

2 About Me Complete the sentences about this unit.

1 I can talk about ______ .

2 I can write about ______ .

3 My favourite part is ______ .

3 Puzzle Guess what it is.

You need an umbrella for this weather. What is it?

______

Go to page 93 and write the answer.

Review Units 7 and 8

1 Think Look and write.

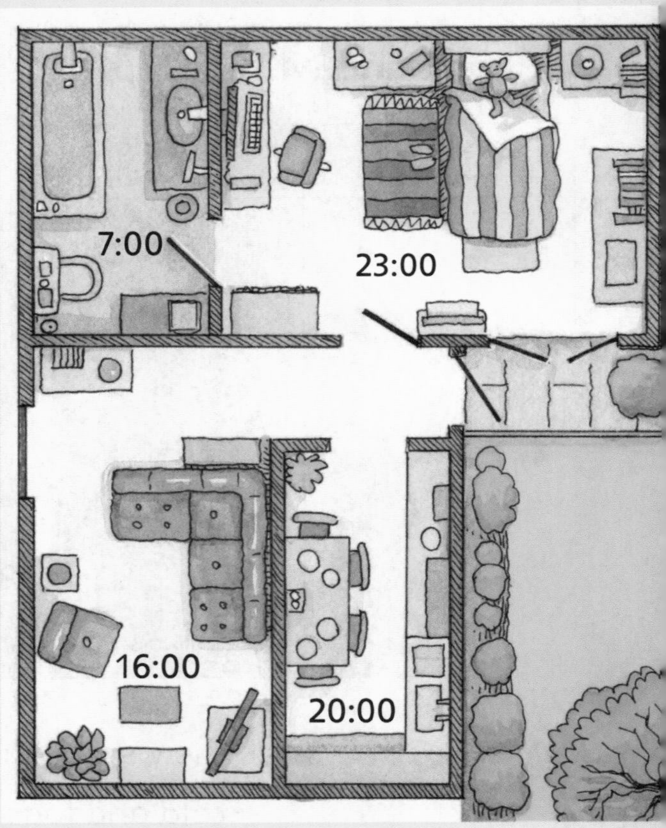

7:00
23:00
16:00
20:00

1 Where *were you* yesterday?
I was at home.

2 Where __________ yesterday morning?
__________ in the __________ .

3 Where __________ yesterday afternoon?
__________ in the __________ .

4 Where __________ yesterday evening?
__________ in the __________ .

5 __________ last night?
__________ in my __________ .

2 Look and write.

1 

SHOP

Were you at the shopping centre in the afternoon?
Yes, I was.

2 

__________ at the cinema yesterday afternoon?
____

3 

__________ at home yesterday morning?
____

3 About Me Answer the questions.

1 Where were you yesterday morning? __________
2 Where were you yesterday afternoon? __________
3 Where were you yesterday evening? __________
4 Where were you last night? __________

4 Look and write.

yesterday

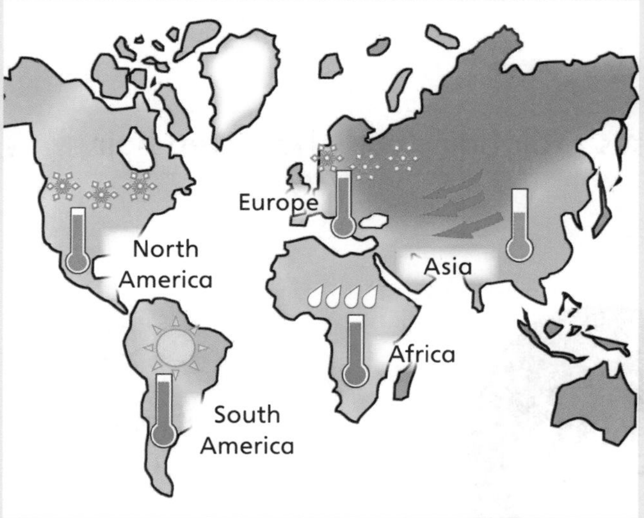
Europe
North America
Asia
Africa
South America

today

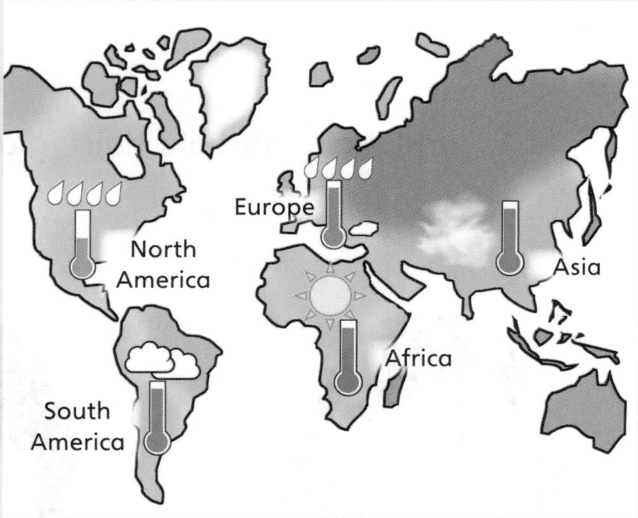
Europe
North America
Asia
Africa
South America

1 ___What's___ the weather like in Africa today?

It's hot and sunny.

2 ___What was___ the weather like in Africa yesterday?

It was hot and rainy.

3 ______________ the weather like in North America today?

____

4 ______________ the weather like in North America yesterday?

____

5 ______________ the weather like in Asia today?

____

6 ______________ the weather like in Asia yesterday?

____

7 ______________ the weather like in South America today?

____

8 ______________ the weather like in South America yesterday?

____

Welcome back!

dark hair straight hair glasses fair hair ~~curly hair~~ red hair

curly hair

1 Fun sports

ice skating sailing skiing kayaking skateboarding fishing
~~bowling~~ mountain biking snowboarding

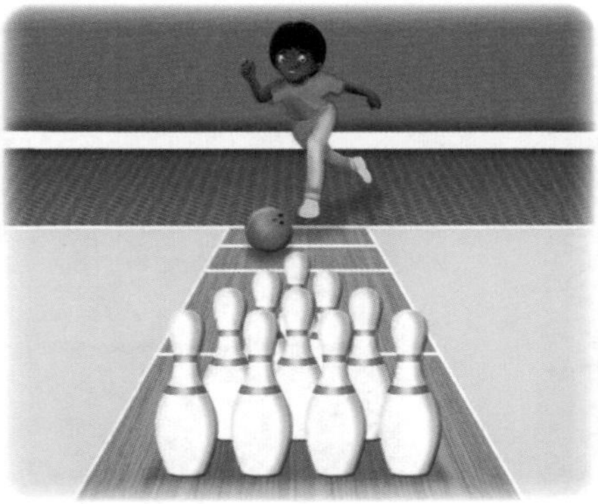

bowling

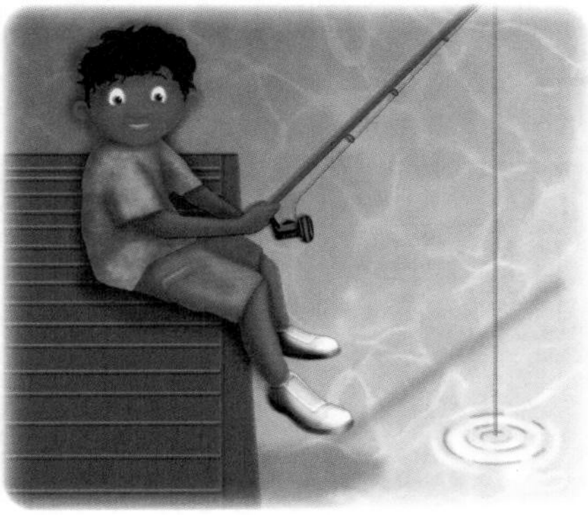

2 Around town

traffic light museum hotel underground station shopping centre
bus station zebra crossing square ~~bank~~ restaurant

€£$

bank

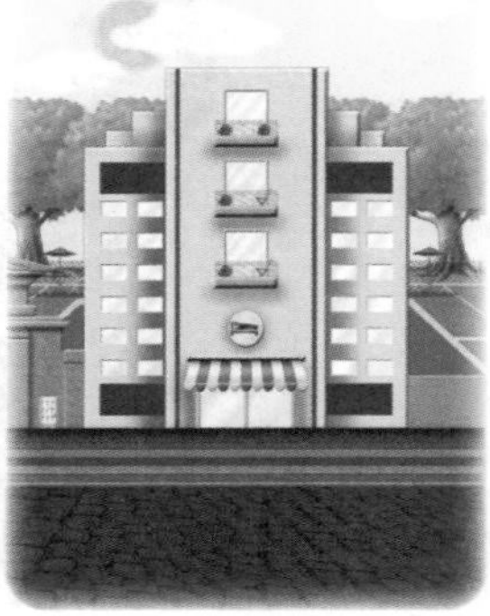

3 At work

vet ~~actor~~ singer doctor pilot businesswoman
artist bus driver nurse businessman

actor

____

____

____

____

____

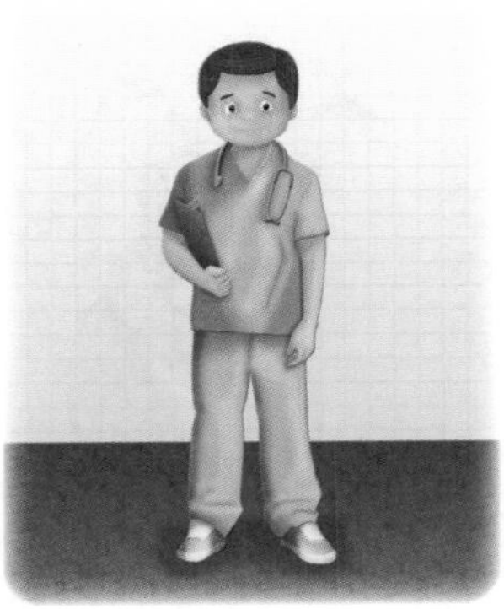

____

____

____

____

4 Wild animals

parrot gorilla owl koala panda jaguar ~~bat~~ penguin kangaroo bear

bat

5 Food and drink

~~biscuit~~ pizza pasta crisps nuts coffee soup tea salad yoghurt

biscuit

6 Health matters

temperature ~~backache~~ cold headache cough
stomachache sore throat earache toothache

backache ______

______

______

______

______

______

______

______

______

7 Buildings

stairs basement third floor roof ~~attic~~ second floor
lift garage ground floor first floor

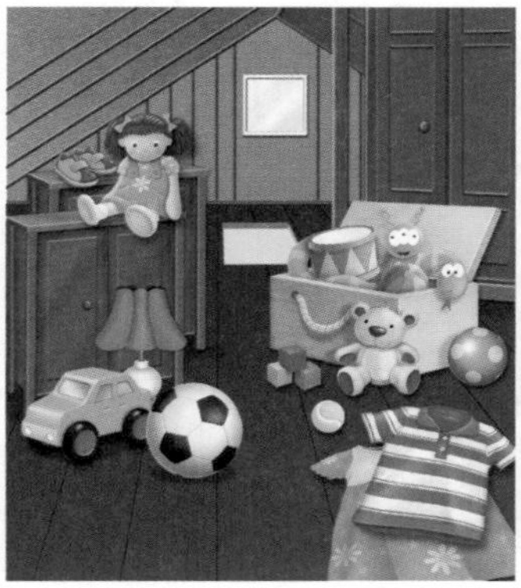

attic

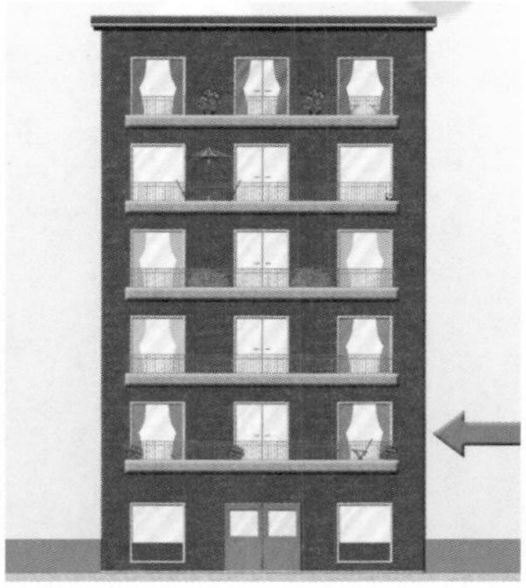

10

0

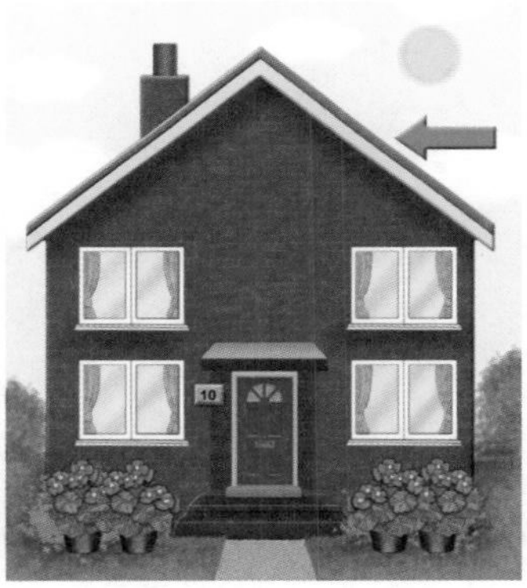

10

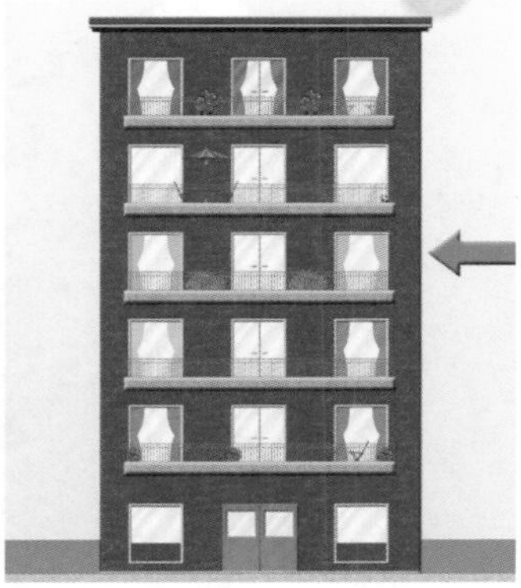

8 Weather

foggy snowy hot rainy warm windy ~~cold~~ cloudy sunny

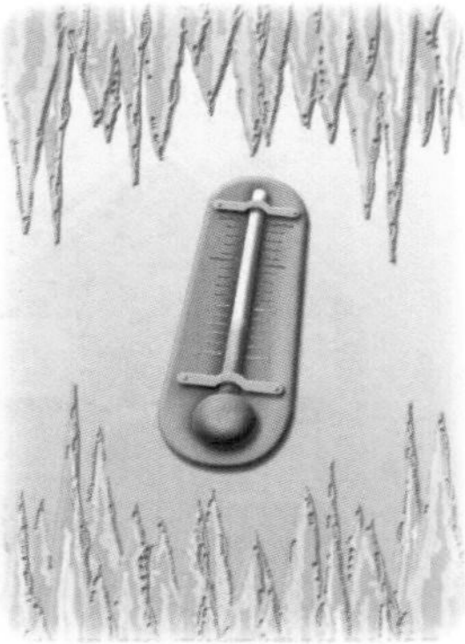

cold

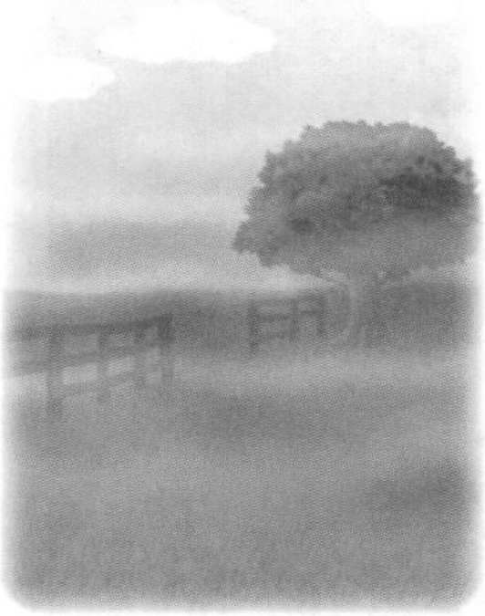

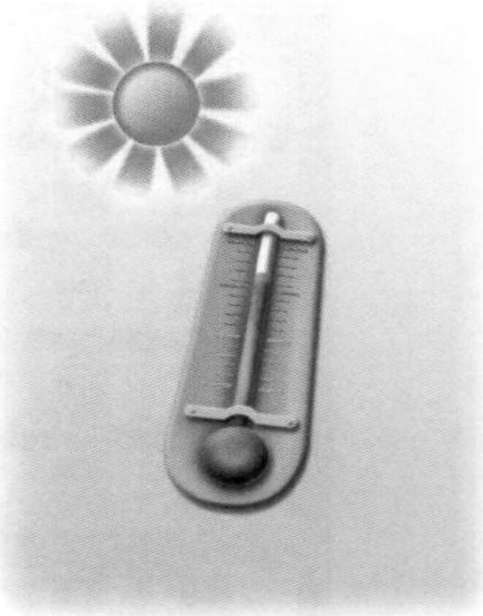

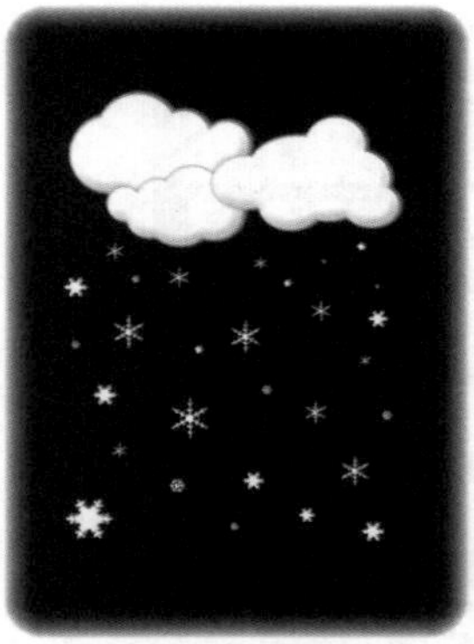

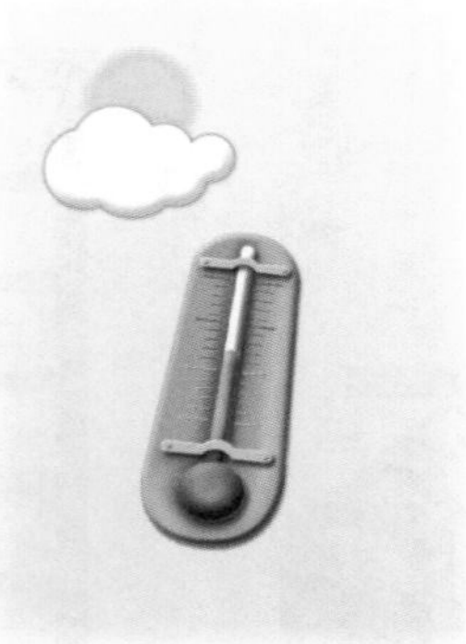

Puzzle

1 Do the word puzzle.

Across →

3 **(Unit 4)** It's big and black and white. It eats leaves. What is it?
4 **(Welcome back!)** Hair that's not straight. What is it?
5 **(Unit 6)** Eating a lot of food can give you a … What is it?
7 **(Unit 1)** You need water and wind to do this sport. What is it?
8 **(Unit 7)** It's quicker than the stairs. What is it?

Down ↓

1 **(Unit 8)** You need an umbrella for this weather. What is it?
2 **(Unit 2)** You stop when it's red. You go when it's green. What is it? (two words)
3 **(Unit 3)** This person can fly a helicopter. Who is it?
6 **(Unit 5)** It's a drink. It's dark brown. It's usually hot. It's not tea. What is it?

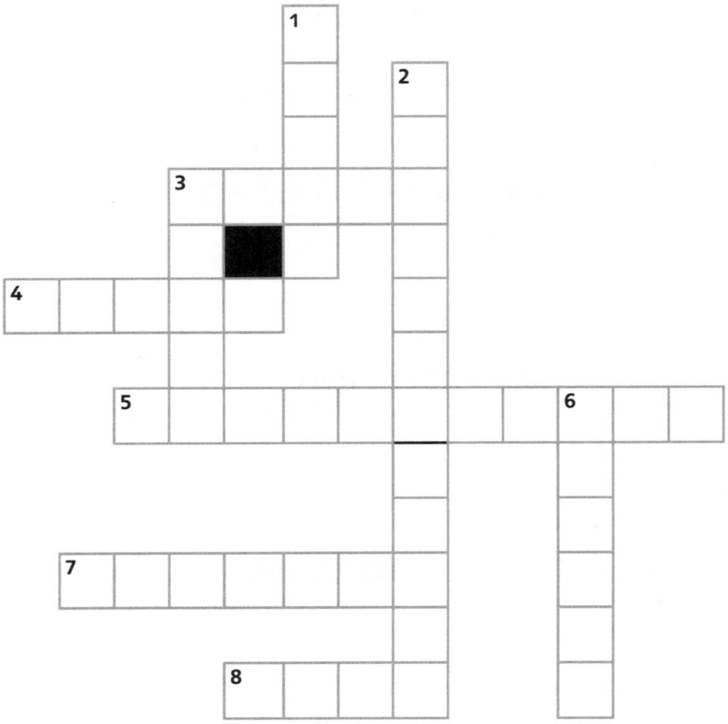
1
2
3
4
5
6
7
8

Story fun

1 Match the objects to the words. Then match the words to the story units they come from.

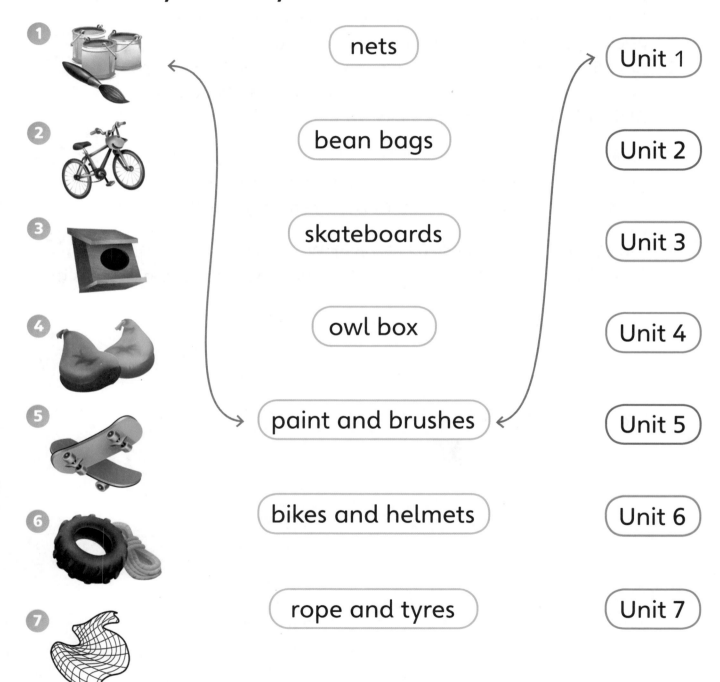

1 

2 

3 

4 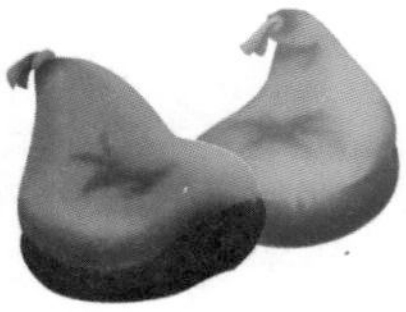

5 

6 

7 

- nets
- bean bags
- skateboards
- owl box
- paint and brushes
- bikes and helmets
- rope and tyres

- Unit 1
- Unit 2
- Unit 3
- Unit 4
- Unit 5
- Unit 6
- Unit 7

2 Look and find the missing people and objects. Write the numbers in the boxes.

1

1

2

3

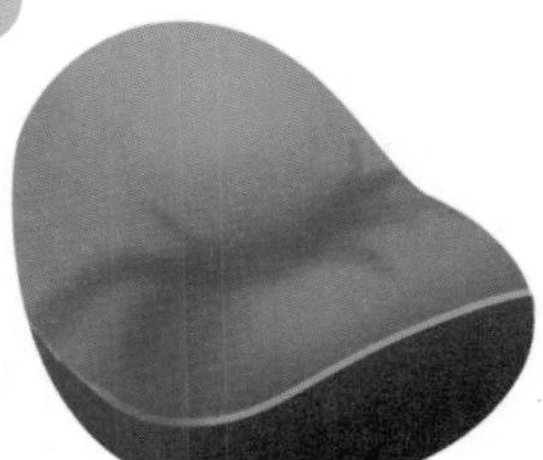

4

5

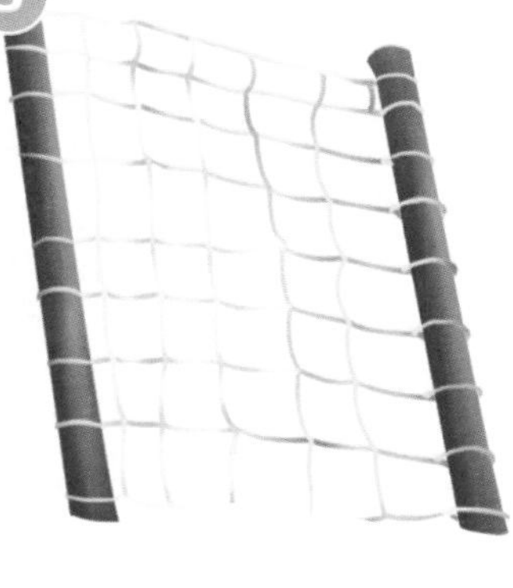

6

7